Figuratively Speaking

For FF
Atrani, Fall 1986

Designed by James J. Johnson
and set in Bodoni Roman types by Delmas, Ann Arbor, Michigan.
Printed in the United States of America by Murray Printing Company,
Westford, Massachusetts.

Library of Congress Cataloging-in-Publication Data

Fogelin, Robert J.
    Figuratively speaking.

    Bibliography: p.
    Includes index.
    1. Figures of speech.   2. Metaphor.   I. Title.
PN227.F57   1988   808   87–34514
ISBN 0–300–04229–9 (alk. paper)

The paper in this book meets the guidelines for permanence and dura-
bility of the Committee on Production Guidelines for Book Longevity of
the Council on Library Resources.

10   9   8   7   6   5   4   3   2   1

Figuratively Speaking

ROBERT J. FOGELIN

YALE UNIVERSITY PRESS

NEW HAVEN AND LONDON

Contents

Preface

Though they appear first, prefaces are always written last, often in a make-believe future tense. This preface is backward looking: it is intended to thank those who have helped bring this work to completion.

Since various parts of this essay have been presented in different stages of development to a number of audiences, it is not possible to acknowledge all my debts. I have learned a great deal from discussions that have followed these presentations, as I have from conversations with my colleagues in the Dartmouth Philosophy Department.

Throughout this essay I have tried to test my ideas concerning figurative language against rich and complex literary texts, and in doing so I have come to appreciate the possibilities for alternative readings of these texts. Here I have profited particularly from conversations with Stanley Eveling and Florence Fogelin.

Ted Cohen, someone I have met only once, and then only briefly, read the complete manuscript with sympathy and care and made important suggestions for its improvement. At various points I have tried to acknowledge his contributions, but some of his most important suggestions must remain unacknowledged since we do not have a convention for thanking people for things they have persuaded us not to say.

I also wish to thank Jane Taylor and Judith Calvert for their help in copyediting the text, and Jeanne Ferris of Yale University Press for her support in bringing this slim volume into print.

Publication of this work was supported by grants from the Faculty Research Committee and the Dean of the Faculty Office of Dartmouth College.

1

Introduction

This work concerns figures of speech, but not all of them. I shall not examine *hyperbation* or any of those other figures (*anaphora, symploce,* et cetera) that concern word order, patterns of repetition, and the like. Their use, for example, in the speeches of Martin Luther King, Jr., shows their lasting power, and it would be interesting to know how these syntactical, seemingly mechanical figures achieve this power. I shall not, however, discuss them here because they are not connected with *meaning* in the way that interests me.

Using the current critical vocabulary, I might say that I am interested in *tropes* as opposed to *schemes* (figures of thought as opposed to figures of sound), but given the controversies that surround these terms, that distinction could prove misleading as well. One issue, which most philosophers would find hard to take seriously, is whether Cicero was right in restricting tropes to single word substitutions. Of more systematic interest is the question whether it is possible to draw a sharp distinction between figures that concern meaning (tropes) and those that do not (schemes). The answer is probably no, but I do not want to get involved in this issue either. Finally, tropes are often defined in a way that runs counter to one of the fundamental ideas of this essay. Lanham describes current critical usage this way:

> Such consensus as there is wants trope to mean a figure that changes the meaning of a word or words, rather than simply arranging them in a pattern of some sort. (101)

Over against this, I shall argue that in most of those figures traditionally called tropes, literal meaning is preserved rather than altered.[1]

There are also figures of speech that do concern meaning rather than patterns of word order, which still fall outside the scope of this study. In *onomatopoeia*, for example, words are chosen in such a way that their sound reflects the meaning of what is said. But I shall not discuss this figure either because meaning, here, is not the source of figurativeness in the way that concerns me. Generally—and the exceptions are interesting and will be examined in detail—I am primarily concerned with those figures of speech that relate to meaning in a way that bears upon the *truth* of what is asserted.

Irony presents a clear example of a figure that functions in the way that concerns me. Reflecting upon his government's tendency to develop oppressive institutions opposite in character from the ideals they were supposed to embody, a Romanian intellectual remarked, "We would have done better to seek a fascist state." It is clear, if not altogether easy to paraphrase, what the person is getting at, and he is certainly not expressing a preference for fascism. If asked bluntly "Do you really believe that?" he would probably blink in disbelief at the naiveté of the question, but still, the answer to it would be no.

---

1. In a suitably broad sense of *meaning* that might include standard conversational implications, it might make sense to say that tropes involve meaning shifts. Still, this would not involve a shift in the *literal meaning of words*, which is what the traditional theorists seemed to have in mind.

Irony is one paradigm of the kind of figure of speech I shall examine. Clustered around it are other figures, including *hyperbole* and *meiosis*, which I have collectively labeled, perhaps not well, *figurative predications*. They are the subject of chapter 2.

Similes and metaphors are paradigms of a second family of figures of speech that I have labeled, somewhat tendentiously, *figurative comparisons*.[2] *Allegories*, some *analogies*, and perhaps *parodies* and *burlesques*, belong here as well. With particular emphasis on similes and metaphors, these figures are discussed in detail in chapters 3 through 6.

A word about the methodological commitments of this work: I have tried to make them transparent and keep them to a minimum. At various places I rely on the theory of speech acts developed by J. L. Austin, and elaborated by John Searle, Ted Cohen, myself, and others. From H. P. Grice, I have taken over the idea, crucial for this study, that communication (both direct and indirect) depends upon the mutual recognition of intentions between speaker and respondent.

In adopting these ideas, I have not, however, taken over the detailed theoretical frameworks in which they were developed. For example, one of the leading ideas of speech-act theory is that using a language is a rule-governed purposive activity. Thus to understand a particular use of language, we should ask what purpose it is intended to achieve and, correlated with this, what rules govern it. Beyond this general commitment, Austin sketched an elaborate theory of the levels or dimensions of speech acts in terms of locutionary, illocutionary, and perlocutionary acts (93ff.). John Searle's *Speech Acts* and subsequent writings present another detailed realization of the general strategy of a speech-act theory. In saying that I have tried to keep my methodological commitments to a minimum, part of what I mean is that my

---

2. The label is tendentious since many philosophers, as we shall see in chapter 3, now deny that metaphors express comparisons.

---

arguments will not depend on the fine-grained features of one realization of the general strategy of a speech-act theory over some other.

Parallel remarks hold for my borrowings from Grice.[3] Once it is pointed out that communication depends upon a mutual recognition of intentions between speaker and respondent, it is hard to imagine that anyone would want to deny this. Furthermore, it is easy to show that this mutual recognition of intentions is crucial for indirect uses of language, including the figurative uses of language, examined in this work. We can acknowledge this much, however, without further supposing that mutually recognized intentions provide the central concept for a *general* account of meaning. I confess to having sympathy with Grice's program, despite its well known difficulties, of defining speaker's meaning in terms of mutually recognized intentions, and then defining sentence (or word) meaning in terms of speaker's meaning, but nothing in this work relies upon the success of this program.

I have no lumpen-Wittgensteinian prejudices against *theories of language*, but this work is not an attempt to further such a theory. This work is about figures of speech; they are not discussed in the service of some larger project.

3. Two of H. P. Grice's classic essays have been particularly important to me: "Logic and Conversation" and "Meaning." His ideas are developed in more depth in his "Utterer's Meaning, Sentence-Meaning and Word-Meaning" and "Utterer's Meaning and Intentions."

2

Figurative Predications

How do ironic utterances work? One explanation has been given
by H. P. Grice:

> X, with whom till now A has been on close terms, has
> betrayed a secret of A's to a business rival. A and his
> audience both know this. A says "X is a fine friend."
> (Gloss: It is perfectly obvious to A and his audience that
> what A has said or has made as if to say is something
> which he does not believe, and the audience knows that
> A knows that this is obvious to the audience. So, unless
> A's utterance is entirely pointless, A must be trying to get
> across some proposition other than the one he purports to
> be putting forward. This must be some obviously related
> proposition; the most obviously related proposition is the
> contradictory of the one he purports to be putting for-
> ward.) ("Conversation" 53)

John Searle says much the same thing:

Stated very crudely, the mechanism by which irony
works is that the utterance, if taken literally, is obviously
inappropriate to the situation. Since it is grossly inappropriate, the hearer is compelled to reinterpret it in such a
way as to render it appropriate, and the most natural way
to interpret it as meaning the opposite of its literal form.
("Metaphor" 113)

These views are close, but not identical. Grice says that the
intended meaning is the *contradictory* of the one the person
purports to be putting forward, whereas Searle makes the seemingly stronger claim that the speaker intends the *opposite* of what
he actually says. This seems stronger, for by the opposite we
usually mean something that lies at the other end of some
scale—for example, big rather than small, none rather than all,
bright rather than dark, and so forth. Who is right? The answer,
as I shall show, is that neither of them is fully right. Sometimes,
though I think rarely, in using an ironic utterance we intend the
contradictory of what we actually say; sometimes we mean the
opposite. In general we imply something incompatible with what
we say, but, as we shall see, the strength of this incompatible
proposition admits of wide variation. One task for a theory of
ironic utterances is to explain what determines which of these
incompatible propositions the use of an ironic sentence conveys.

An account of ironic utterances should answer a second
cluster of questions as well: why do ironic utterances carry
rhetorical force; why do they have clout? Why is irony, along with
other related figures of speech, often used in arguments, even
serious arguments? After all, on the face of it, the pattern for an
ironic utterance should strike us as exceedingly peculiar. We
wish to assert p, and to do this we assert some other proposition,
p^* (say the opposite or contradictory of p). In the imagined
conversational context, the parties mutually know that p^* is false,
because they know that p is true, so they infer that the speaker
really meant to assert p. But isn't this a strange way to carry on? If

someone wants to assert *p*, why not just do it? More perplexing still, if, in the given context, it is mutually known that *p* is true, what is the point of asserting *p* at all, either directly or indirectly? Taken directly, the ironic utterance is false; taken indirectly, it is otiose.

I think that we can make progress in answering both these questions by introducing the notion of a *standard* and *natural response*. By a *standard* response, I mean the kind of response that takes place in most cases and is expected to take place. By a *natural* response, I mean one that does not demand elaborate cogitation. The standard and natural response to a speech act may be an action, a speech act, or a mental act. Furthermore, what the respondent *actually says* may be chained to (or layered on) a response that is not itself expressed. The standard response to a question is, for example, an answer; the response is natural if it can be given more or less straight-off.

RHETORICAL QUESTIONS

The notion of a standard and natural response can help us understand what Grice has called *conversational implication* ("Conversation") and what Searle has called *indirect speech acts* ("Indirect"). Sometimes when we perform a speech act, we antici-pate the content of (what I have called) the standard and natural response, and that response is precisely what we are trying to evoke. (Furthermore, I often intend that this intention be clear to my listener, but I shall come back to this.) What I have in mind can be illustrated by examining the difference between *rhetorical* and *non-rhetorical* questions. Lost, I might ask someone (non-rhetorically), "Is this the road to Wellfleet?" Assuming that I am dealing with a cooperative Cape Codder, the standard and natural response will be a *yes* or *no*. But that answer is not part of my meaning in asking the question for, lost, I do not know the answer to my question. Again lost, I come to a dead-end in the middle of a bog, and a fellow passenger asks "Is this the road to Wellfleet?" Obviously, it is not the road to Wellfleet, since Wellfleet is not a bog. Here the standard answer is a *yes* or a *no* and, in this context, since the facts are plain, the natural response is *no*. The person who asks the question knows that this is the appropriate response, and his point in asking it is to elicit this response. Furthermore, these features are *mutually recognized* by the speaker and respondent. Here we can say that in asking the rhetorical question the person has *conversationally implied, indirectly asserted*, or, in common parlance, *meant* that this is not the road to Wellfleet.

Let me block a possible misunderstanding of the position I am developing. Confronted with the rhetorical question "Is this the road to Wellfleet?" I might reply in a variety of ways. The standard and natural response to this question is *no*, but, reacting to the transparent rhetorical point of the question, I may not say this. Instead, I might react to the accusation implied by the question, and engage in rhetoric of my own, perhaps by saying: "If you're so smart, why didn't you tell us when we made a wrong turn?" Here the reply is chained to the original rhetorical question through the standard and natural response, *no*, and even if not expressed, as is likely, its mutual recognition is needed to account for the connection between the utterances actually made.

Having concentrated on the speaker's intended meaning, I now turn to the force the rhetorical question has on the respondent. The point of the rhetorical question is to elicit the response (in speech, if possible; in thought, at least) that this emphatically is not the road to Wellfleet. Rhetorical questions gain their force by making the questioner's indirect speech act the respondent's direct speech (or, at least, thought) act. We do this for a variety of reasons. In the present case, the rhetorical question gains its force from the principle that, in general, admissions are worth more than accusations.[1]

A parallel account is possible for ironic utterances. The standard response to assertions is to accept them or reject them. For example, the standard response to what we take to be a false statement is to deny it. Furthermore, in a particular context, it is natural to provide the correct judgment in its place. If *A* falsely says, "I've paid you that money," *B* might reply, "No you haven't; you still owe me $10." The exact form of *B*'s corrective response will depend upon the setting in which the remark is made. The same situation obtains for the use of ironic utterances. *A* says something false, and *B*, given the momentum of the conversational exchange, provides (in speech or thought) the corrective judgment.

Now, to return to the difference between Grice and Searle noted at the start of this discussion, the form the corrective judgment takes depends upon the context. "Great throw" can have the force of "horrible throw" if that's the proper corrective judgment in the given context (for example, when the shortstop has just thrown the ball into the dirt, wide of first base). But endless variations are possible between the extremes of mere contradiction and the assertion of the complete opposite. Here is one illustrative case: In rehearsal an actor is stumbling over his lines and the director ironically remarks, "I see you have your lines down pat." The remark does not have the force of asserting the complete opposite, namely that he has learned *none* of his lines, for the actor has, after all, learned *some* of them. Yet it has more force than the bare contradictory claim that he has *not* mastered them all, for the irony would be out of place if the actor had only stumbled over a single line. More than likely, the director is indicating that the actor has a long way to go before he

---

1. There are, of course, more benign uses of rhetorical questions. We also use them to be polite or to allow another to draw an obvious inference.

has learned his part. This brings me to my first conclusion about ironic utterances: *The indirect content of an ironic utterance is determined by the corrective judgment that it naturally invokes within the context in which it is made.*[2]

More interestingly, this account helps explain why irony can have bite. Often, though not always, irony is used as a form of criticism, and here the parallel with rhetorical questions is close. With a rhetorical question, the respondent is often led to acknowledge something (in speech or thought) that is to his or her discredit. Similarly, with an ironic utterance, the natural re-

---

2. This conclusion holds for standard contexts where the ironic speaker succeeds in his purpose, but speech acts, like other acts, can also fail. *A*'s stinging irony can be lost on his obtuse respondent *B*. In such a case, I think that we would still say that *A* has spoken ironically because of his intent to call forth a mutually recognized corrective judgment that reverses what was said. More carefully, then, a specification of the indirect content of an ironic utterance should make reference to the speaker's intent to call forth what he or she takes to be a corrective judgment. This consideration points to a range of cases where a figurative utterance can fail in its purpose because of an error on the part of the speaker rather than on the obtuseness of the respondent. Imagine the ironic speaker, unknown to himself, saying something generally taken to be *true*. Again, with a rhetorical question, the standard answer might be the reverse of what the speaker expects. For many years, the question "Is the pope Italian?" was a way of giving an unqualified affirmative answer to some question. Imagine a speaker, somehow ignorant of recent papal history, using this rhetorical question now. (More interestingly, imagine the intended effect of an informed speaker now addressing it to an informed respondent.) A *theory* of ironic utterances (and figurative language in general) would contain a full specification of the way or ways in which the speaker's intentions determine the indirect content of an ironic utterance. In this discussion, however, I am primarily interested in calling attention to the importance of an expected corrective judgment in providing this determination. To carry the analysis further would involve a commitment to a particular (and presumably controversial) version of speech-act theory which, for reasons given in chapter 1, I have tried to avoid. [These reflections were provoked by comments from Ted Cohen.]

sponse is often a corrective judgment critical of the person in whom the response takes place. To the ironic claim, "You're a fine friend," the natural response may be "No I'm not; I really let you down." Now whether the respondent actually says this or only thinks it, it is still an acknowledgment that he might make, perhaps despite himself. Furthermore, what the person actually says is often chained to this natural response. Absorbing the response, he may join in the irony, saying "Yes, I was a real peach." Alternatively, he may bridle and respond aggressively, "As if you're so perfect!"

These last remarks point to a difference in emphasis between the approach taken here and that presented by Grice in his classic paper "Logic and Conversation." One of the central claims of Grice's paper is this:

> The presence of a conversational implicature must be capable of being worked out; for even if it can in fact be intuitively grasped, unless the intuition is replaceable by argument, the implicature (if present at all) will not count as a *conversational* implicature; it will be a *conventional* implicature. (50)

For Grice this calculation, as he sometimes calls it (57–58), will take into account such things as the conventional meaning of the speaker's utterance, the Cooperative Principle and its maxims, the context, background knowledge, and the fact that those participating in the conversation mutually recognize all these things. Grice, as I read him, emphasizes the relationship between the conventional meaning of the utterance and the system of rules that govern it. Sometimes we must appeal to additional contextual information, for example, in order to recognize that a conversational rule is being flouted, but, in general, conversational implication is *calculated* on the basis of two factors: conventional meaning and conversational rules. Over against this, I have suggested that the indirect content of the ironic remark is highly context-dependent since it is provided by the corrective judgment that naturally arises in the conversational exchange.

I now turn to the second question raised at the start of this essay: how do ironic utterances gain their force? Watching a game of pool, *A* (who doesn't understand the rules) sees *B* sink the eight ball and shouts "Great shot!" In fact, *B* sank the eight ball inadvertently and, as a result, has lost. The corrective response to *A*'s remark is that it was not a great shot, but a blunder. For all that, *A*'s remark is not ironic for it was not *intended* to elicit this corrective judgment. It's at this level that Grice's insistence on the importance of mutually recognized intentions finds its place. If it is clear that *A* uttered his remark without the intention of producing a corrective response, then the remark was not ironic. But if the 'praise' was offered with just the intention of invoking this corrective response, where this intention is made clear, then we have irony.

Irony can be manipulative and thus humiliating. Perhaps it is for this reason that irony is often a vehicle for (or at least combined with) sarcasm. Irony is not the only vehicle for sarcasm—rhetorical questions can be asked in a sarcastic tone of voice as well; still, for obvious reasons, irony and sarcasm go well together. In passing, this reference to sarcasm may help avoid a misunderstanding. At certain places I have spoken of irony where others might say that we are dealing with sarcasm. The actor example may strike the reader this way. To the criticism "That's not irony; that's sarcasm," there are two things worth saying. First, a great deal will depend upon how we imagine the context, including the tone of voice. The force of "Well, you've certainly got your lines down pat" can vary from light irony (perhaps intended as a mild joke) to savage criticism. Second, even in cases where a remark is plainly sarcastic, this does not show that it is not also ironic. Calling a sarcastic remark ironic may *underdescribe* it, but it need not *misdescribe* it.

MEIOSIS AND HYPERBOLE

I hold that ironic utterances function by invoking mutually recognized corrective responses. Their *point* is to invoke mutually recognized corrective responses. But this is not a unique feature of ironic judgments, for other figures of speech function in the same way. Consider understatement (meiosis). Here I say something weaker than I am in a position to say; for example, I say that someone has had something to drink when, in fact, he is utterly intoxicated. The corrective judgment goes: "What do you mean he has had *something* to drink? He's plastered." My remark counts as meiosis when it is mutually recognized that I have spoken with the intention of invoking this corrective judgment.[3]

How does irony differ from meiosis? Irony reverses polarity; thus ironic 'praise' becomes blame. My impression is that people will call something understatement if (true or false) it invokes a mutually recognized corrective judgment toward the extreme (on some scale). Understatement does not reverse polarity, but instead invites a *strengthening* correction.

Hyperbole works the other way round. Here I say something stronger than what I have a right to say with the intention of having it corrected away from the extreme, but still to something *strong* that preserves the *same polarity*. When someone claims to be famished, he is typically indicating that he is very hungry. Hyperbole is an exaggeration on the side of the truth. These contrasts are reflected in the following diagram:

3. Euphemism sometimes takes a similar form, though with a different intent. *A* might describe *B*, who has passed out, as having had a bit to drink, not, as with meiosis, in order to emphasize *B*'s drunkenness, but as a way of not saying everything that might be said, as a way, that is, of not being censorious.

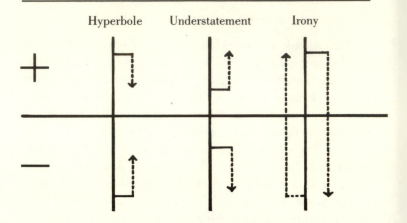

Hyperbole   Understatement   Irony

In passing, this diagram looks similar to one found in Nelson Goodman's *The Languages of Art* (82).

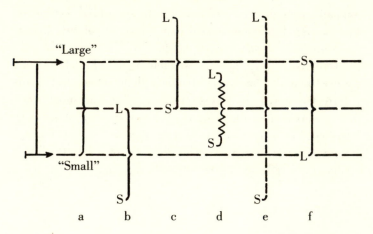

a. b. c. d. e. f.

a. Literal application   c. Understatement   e. Underemphasis
                                              (under/overstatement)

b. Hyperbole   d. Overemphasis   f. Irony
                         (over/understatement)

Goodman's leading idea is that the figures of speech that I have discussed, plus some others, are instances of *metaphors;* indeed, he discusses them under the heading "Modes of Metaphor." For Goodman, a metaphor involves the *transfer* of a *schema*. He describes a schema as a "family" or "set" of labels (71–72). The *range* of a single label is just those objects denoted by it. And "the aggregate of the ranges of extension of the labels in a schema may be called a *realm*" (72). To use his own example, the system of labels used to classify or grade olives exemplifies such a schema, with certain olives making up the range of the label 'supercolossal,' and all the olives sorted by the system of labels constituting the realm of the schema. Turning next to the transfer of schemata, Goodman holds that such transfers of schemata can produce metaphorical (or figurative) language in at least two ways. At times the transfer involves a movement from one realm to another disjoint from it (as for example, in the personification of the weather). At other times the realms are not disjoint, but, instead, "one realm intersects or is an expansion or contraction of the other" (81). Applying this second idea to figures of speech, he continues:

> In hyperbole, for instance, an ordered schema is displaced downward. The large olive becomes a supercolossal and the small one large. . . . In litotes, or understatement, exactly the opposite occurs. A superb performance becomes pretty fair and a good one passable. (81–83)

His diagram indicates that in irony an ordered schema is flip-flopped.

I have a simple objection to this elegant theory: it doesn't seem true to the facts. I think that Goodman is right in saying that an entire ordered schema can be displaced hyperbolically, but this hardly seems to serve as a general account of the way hyperbole works. When I say that a particular throw was the worst that I have seen in my life (when it wasn't), I do not displace any other judgments about the game; medium-fast pitches, for example, are not now considered the fastest (or should it be the slowest?) that I have ever seen delivered. In most cases, the hyperbole stops with the single remark and the corrective response it calls forth. Typically, there is no broader displacement of the kind that Goodman suggests. The same point holds against Goodman's account of irony. Although we might invert an entire schema for ironic purposes, in fact, for the most part, irony does not involve such a wholesale inversion of a schema. [4]

I have spoken about meiosis, irony, and hyperbole as contrasting figures of speech. This does not mean that they cannot be used to achieve similar ends. In fact, often, all three devices are simultaneously available to make the same indirect claim. At the Battle of Jutland, Admiral Beatty, on seeing two of his battle cruisers blown out of the water in rapid succession, is reported to have said: "Chatfield, there seems to be something wrong with our bloody ships today." Never has understatement better served the purposes of unflappability. Beatty might also have spoken with bitter irony, saying "Good show." And hyperbole was also available: "Chatfield, you have just witnessed the end of Western civilization as we know it." In each case, the speaker says something mutually understood to be in need of correction. The indirect content of these figures of speech is given by the form of the corrective judgment. That the utterance counts as a figure of speech is grounded in the fact that the parties engaged mutually understand that a corrective judgment is being invoked.

---

4. I also have deep reservations about Goodman's treatment of metaphors themselves, and shall return to this issue when I examine various theories of metaphor in chapter 5.

SOME QUALIFICATIONS AND ELABORATIONS

On the assumption that I have offered a tolerably good account of the *routine* uses of irony and related figures of speech, I would now like to introduce some qualifications and elaborations in order to do more justice to the complexity and subtlety of these uses of language.

First the qualifications. The leading idea is that the figures of speech I have examined function by invoking a *mutually recognized standard and natural corrective response*. Here a brief warning about the word 'corrective' is in order. This word may suggest censure or criticism, and, in fact, as my examples have tended to show, irony is often used for these purposes. But here I wish to use it in the more neutral sense of *setting something right*. With all these figures of speech, an utterance is made with the mutually recognized intention that the respondent will naturally *adjust* the utterance in an appropriate way.

I should also acknowledge that it is misleading to suggest, as my examples have tended to suggest, that these corrections or adjustments always involve the truth of some utterance. We can say things in (mutually recognized) need of correction without *asserting* anything. Congratulations (even applause) can be ironic. Different kinds of speech acts will admit of different patterns of correction, but I shall not examine this topic here.

Concentrating on irony, some elaborations. So far I have largely dwelled on a single, quite common, case: *A* utters something ironic to *B*, and *B*, in producing a corrective judgment, acknowledges something unpleasant about himself. Here the *respondent to* and the *target of* the ironic utterance are the same. But a person can also speak with self-irony. Having betrayed *B*, *A* might say to him, "Well, I am a fine friend," where *A* and *B* mutually recognize that this utterance will invoke a corrective judgment in conflict with it. Here *A*'s ironic remark, by inviting a criticism, amounts to a confession. *A* can also speak ironically to *B* about some third party *C*.

17

It is also sometimes useful to draw a distinction between the *addressee* of an ironic remark and those other respondents who are not addressees. (*C* has let *B* down and *A* says to *B*, in *C*'s presence, "*C* is certainly a fine friend." Here both *C* and *B* are respondents, but only *B* is the addressee.) Finally, out of the class of respondents, some may be naive, others informed. *A* may speak ironically to naive *B* for the general amusement of a sophisticated third party *C*. Thus Mark Twain offered elaborate praise for the doggerel verse of Sarah Orne Jewett, much to the amusement of his intellectual friends. The pleasure was, of course, heightened by the thought that Sarah Orne Jewett would fail to detect the irony. Through all these cases, the same underlying mechanism appears: *A* utters something with the mutually understood intention of inducing a corrective judgment in an informed respondent. In itself, the mechanism of irony is simple; its subtlety arises from the levels of mutual recognition possible among informed participants in a linguistic exchange.

DIFFICULTIES

I do not want to give the impression that I have given a complete analysis of irony (or any of the other related figures of speech), for there are many interesting cases that I still find baffling. For example, alone reading something I have published, I discover that it is riddled with typographical errors that I had missed in proof. I say to myself, "Eagle-eye Fogelin has done it again." Here a metaphor is used ironically, but it is not clear how the irony works. I am the utterer of the ironic remark. I am also the addressee, an informed respondent, and the target of the ironic remark. But as the person who produces the remark with an ironic intent, I know already that it is false, and I am not trying to produce any corrective or adjusting response in my audience (namely me!). A glib, though perhaps correct, way of dealing with such cases of privately expressed (or closet) self-irony, is to say that the things we call irony form a *family*, and we consider closet self-irony a form of irony because it has so much in common with other more standard cases of irony. I am inclined to think, however, that my analysis does fit the present case. When I use self-irony, I, of course, recognize that I am saying something false and that drives me, as it usually drives others, to acknowledge or face up to an appropriate truth. I realize that I do not mean what I am saying, and I say it with the aim of producing a tension between what I say and what I know to be true. The oddity here does not consist in the way the ironic remark functions, but in the curious, seemingly two-part, relationship which I to take to myself when engaged in self-mockery, self-congratulation, self-irony, and self-deception.

A second difficulty with my analysis arises because we not only speak of ironic utterances, but also of ironic events. Given my analysis, that should seem perplexing since in these cases there is no speech act of any kind that stands in need of correction or adjustment. By an ironic utterance I shall mean (and have meant) an utterance made with the intention of being ironic. Now ironic events, like ironic utterances, exhibit significant reversals of the appropriate or expected, but they do not occur with that intention and often they exhibit no intention at all.[5] For example, it was ironic that a survivor of the bloody landings at Omaha Beach died there twenty-five years later at a ceremony commemorating that landing. It is ironic because he did not die when he most reasonably or appropriately might have and did die when he should not have. It may also seem ironic that he died celebrating,

5. Here D. C. Meucke distinguishes *instrumental irony* from *observable irony*. He also speaks of the *irony of events*, by which he means reversals that take place in a series of events, for example, in the attempt at poisoning, the would-be poisoner poisons himself. My ironic utterances correspond to his instrumental ironies; what I call ironic events, he calls observable ironies; and his irony *of* events is a subclass of what I call ironic events (56ff.).

among other things, the fact that he had not died in that very place. A situation that involves *poetic justice* seems to be a special case of an ironic event where vice is punished or virtue rewarded in a way that is *fitting* or *just*, as the result of an ironic reversal. The standard example is the poisoner who accidentally poisons himself. A better example is the notorious hanging judge who accidentally strangles himself while tying his cravat.[6]

Typically, ironic events do not involve utterances, but they can, for the *fact* that someone says something can itself be ironic. An example from Meucke illustrates this: In the twenty-first book of the *Odyssey*, the suitors (who do not recognize him) are observing Odysseus examining the bow he had left behind more than twenty years earlier; one of them remarks, "Ha! Quite the expert, with a critic's eye for bows! No doubt he collects them at home or wants to start a factory, etc."[7] It is ironic that the suitor said this, though, of course, he is not speaking ironically.

Ironic events share certain features with ironic utterances. In each case there is a reversal of the appropriate that brings forth the response that something that happened or was said should not have happened or been said. The difference between the two cases is, of course, that the intentions (usually mutually recognized intentions) essential to ironic utterances are usually missing in ironic events. Perhaps attributions of irony to events or sequences of events always involve personification, and in that way, intention is again presupposed. (Think of the irony of fate.) And, again, the old *family resemblance* dodge is available; we call events ironic because they share many crucial features with ironic utterances. I am inclined to think that calling an event ironic does involve personification, but I am not sure.

6. This example comes from Timothy Duggan.
7. Cited by Meucke, 14.

DRAMATIC IRONY

Finally, in closing, let me say a few programmatic things about dramatic irony. Dramatic irony can arise in two ways: *internally*, irony can be portrayed within the text, or *externally*, the text itself can be intended ironically. Starting with portrayals of the ironic, a story may spin out the ironic unfolding of events: in "The Gift of the Magi" a husband sells his watch to buy his wife an elegant comb while she sells her hair to buy him a gold chain for his watch—that sort of thing. A text can also represent ironic exchanges, as Plato's early dialogues often do. As far as I can see, dramatic irony in the sense of portraying the ironic raises no special problems.

Ironic portrayals, as opposed to portrayals of the ironic, are more interesting. The author presents a text that is mutually recognized as in need of correction and its mutually recognized point is to call forth this recognition. Satires, parodies, and burlesques fall into this category. In each case the reader is supposed to see that the text, if read straight, is defective. Texts of this kind advertise their defects and then, by analogy, the defects are ascribed to the targets of the irony.

In ironic writing of this kind, the author stands in an ironic relationship to his audience and that relationship can admit of all the variations cataloged above. The audience (or some significant part of it) may be the target of the irony. Think of Swift's *Modest Proposal*. In cahoots with his audience, the author may target some third party for his irony. In a marvelously subtle case of this, dissidents sometimes write disingenuously in order to slip their writing past naive government censors with the intention that sophisticated readers will recognize and appreciate this disingenuousness.

Interesting relationships can emerge between the internal irony of a text and the ironic relationship between the author and his audience. In the early Socratic dialogue the *Euthydemus*,

Plato has Socrates utter ironic remarks that are wholly unappreciated by the other participants in the dialogue. Internal to the dialogue, Socrates speaks ironically only for his own amusement; externally, Plato has him speak this way for our amusement. Here the target is within the dialogue, whereas the intended sophisticated respondents (that's us) are outside it.[8]

A similar but more subtle use of irony to establish a relationship between author and reader occurs in the opening sentence of Jane Austen's *Pride and Prejudice*.

> It is a truth universally acknowledged, that a single man
> in possession of a good fortune must be in want of a wife.

The author, who is both a narrator and commentator, knows, and expects the reader to realize that she knows, that this is not "a truth universally acknowledged." In particular, as the author herself points out in the next sentence, it is not a truth acknowledged by every "single man in possession of a good fortune." Here the author expresses ironically a view that dominates the lives of a number of characters in the narrative to come, and in doing so establishes an understanding with her readers concerning these characters.[9]

8. Of course, there is an external target of the irony as well, that is, those who resemble the characters within the dialogue.

9. Ted Cohen has pointed out that this sentence may also play upon a possible double meaning in the expression "in want of a wife." Florence Fogelin has suggested that it might better be read as an instance of hyperbole rather than irony. The choice between a reading as irony and a reading as hyperbole turns upon the question whether the conversational point of the remark is to call attention to instances that violate it, or to call our attention to its *general* truth, even if it is not, strictly speaking, *universally* true. While the immediate context seems to favor an ironic reading, the single-minded dedication of so many of the characters in the novel to this principle makes a reading as hyperbole plausible as well.

This discussion of irony, hyperbole, and meiosis has turned upon a number of simple ideas. These tropes, in being figurative modes of discourse, depart from, and often violate, our rules for normal ways of speaking. They gain their rhetorical force by inducing a mutually recognized correction or adjustment in the respondent, and the indirect content of each trope is determined by this mutually recognized corrective judgment. In the chapters that follow, I shall offer an account of metaphors, similes, and other figurative comparisons that parallels the discussion in this chapter in stressing the respondent's participatory role in making sense of the figurative utterance. Again, I shall argue that the respondent is called upon to make a correction or adjustment, but, as we shall see, the patterns of correction or adjustment are significantly different from those examined in this chapter.[10]

10. A shorter version of the material in this chapter was presented at the International Conference on Argumentation held in Amsterdam in 1986 and subsequently published in the *Proceedings of the Conference on Argumentation*, vol. 1, *Argumentation Across Lines of Discipline*, eds. Frans H. van Eemen, Rob Grootendorst, J. Anthony Blair, and Charles A. Willard (Dordrecht Forris, 1987).

3

Figurative Comparisons:
The Traditional View

During the past thirty years, there has been a remarkable growth of interest in metaphors. Furthermore, even though theories have come in a variety of competing forms and have been written from various perspectives, one doctrine has achieved a remarkable consensus: Aristotle notwithstanding, metaphors do not assert similarities or make comparisons. Against these united voices, I shall defend the traditional Aristotelian position. Similes wear their comparative form on their grammatical sleeves, and metaphors, I shall argue, differ from similes in only a trivial grammatical way: metaphors are similes with the term of comparison suppressed; they are elliptical similes.

This position is found in Aristotle, though in a somewhat ambiguous form:

> The simile is also a metaphor. The difference is but slight. When the poet says of Achilles that he
>
> Leapt on the foes as a lion
>
> this is simile; when he says of him 'the lion leapt,' it is metaphor . . . [Similes] are to be employed just as meta-

phors are employed, since they are really the same thing except for the difference mentioned. (*Rhetoric* 1406b)

To avoid misunderstandings, it is important to recognize the type of construction that Aristotle takes as paradigmatic when he speaks of a metaphor. In the example he presents, Achilles is *referred to as a lion rather than called* a lion. That is, the construction looks like this:

1. The lion [i.e., Achilles] leapt.

rather than this:

2. Achilles is a lion.

Both Cicero and Quintilian, perhaps following Aristotle, also cite constructions of this first type in their discussion of metaphors. Thus Cicero says:

a metaphor is a brief similitude contracted into a single word; which word being put in the place of another, as it were in its own place, conveys, if the resemblance is acknowledged, delight, if there is no resemblance, it is condemned. (*De Oratore* 3.38.156–39.157)

And Quintilian tells us that a metaphor is a

shorter form of simile, while in the latter we compare some object to the thing which we wish to describe, whereas in the former the object is actually substituted for the thing. (*Institutio Oratoria*, Bk. VIII, vi, 8–9)

Given modern semantical conventions, this may sound peculiar, but the point made by Aristotle, Cicero, and Quintilian is clear: thinking of examples of type (1), they are saying that metaphors provide an alternative way of expressing a simile by *referring* to something using a referring term that literally refers to something else.

Construction (2) above presents a pattern of metaphor more

commonly discussed in recent literature (for example, "Juliet is the sun" and "Sally is a block of ice").[1] Finally, in a third pattern, we speak of something *as if* it were another thing. With apologies for the collapse of poetic diction, the following serves as an example of this:

3. Achilles could hardly wait to get his claws into Hector.

In all three of these cases, a comparison is drawn elliptically that might have been drawn directly.

But even if these writers treat metaphors as elliptical similes, Aristotle, at least, saw that sometimes a metaphor can have more rhetorical force than a simile.

> The simile, as has been said before, is a metaphor, differing from it only in the way it is put; and just because it is longer it is less attractive. Besides, it does not say outright that 'this' *is* 'that,' and therefore the hearer is less interested in the idea. We see, then, that both speech and reasoning are lively in proportion as they make us seize a new idea promptly. (1410b, 11–21)

Metaphors can have more force than their counterpart similes, first, because of their brevity, and that can be more than a matter of one fewer word. There is not much saving in "Achilles is a lion" over "Achilles is like a lion," but considerable saving in "The lion leapt" over "Achilles leapt like a lion." The second difference is more important: metaphors are more startling because, on a superficial reading, they can seem false. (Imagine someone saying: "That wasn't a lion that leapt; it was the man Achilles.") The respondent must reject this reading in favor of a reading as an implicit comparison, and part of the force of a metaphor is to induce just this response.

1. Quintilian speaks of metaphors of this kind as well:

It is a comparison when I say that a man did something *like a lion,* it is a metaphor when I say of him, *He is a lion* (Bk. VIII, vi, 8–9).

Again, in the first passage from Aristotle, although he obviously puts forward an elliptical-simile view of metaphors, the opening sentence seems to place the emphasis the other way around by saying, not that metaphors are (elliptical) similes, but, instead, that "the simile is also a metaphor." Here Aristotle seems to be using the term 'metaphor' in a broad generic sense as a way of indicating that similes are also figures of speech, differing from the metaphors just cited only by expressing their comparison explicitly.[2] Read this way, Aristotle's position comes to this: *Metaphors are figurative comparisons. So are similes. The difference between them is that the comparison is made explicitly in the simile, but not in the metaphor.* I think that this is the most natural way of reading these passages from Aristotle, but, in any case, it is the position I will attempt to elaborate, clarify, and defend in detail. It is the position that I have in mind when I speak of the *elliptical-simile* or the *comparativist* view of metaphors.

Since I shall argue a number of times that attacks upon the comparativist view of metaphors rest on a misrepresentation of that position, let me state, quite simply, what that position comes

2. This tendency to use the term 'metaphor' in a generic way that covers a wide range of tropes and also in a specific way as the name of a particular trope is common practice in both recent and traditional literature. It was commented on explicitly by the seventeenth-century French rhetorician Bernard Lamy:

> Tropes are words transported from their proper significations, and applied to things that they signifie but obliquely. So that all Tropes are *Metaphors* or Translations, according to the Etymology of the Word. And yet by the Figure of *Antonomasia* we give the name of *Metaphor* to a particular Trope, and according to that definition, a *Metaphor* is a Trope by which we put a strange and remote word for a proper word, by reason of its resemblance with the thing of which we speak. (215)

To avoid confusion, I shall not use the term 'metaphor' in this broad generic sense without explicit warning.

to. A person committed to the comparativist account of metaphors will hold at least these two theses:

I. The *literal* meaning of a metaphor of the form 'A is a φ' is the same as the *literal* meaning of the counterpart simile of the form 'A is like a φ.'

II. The *figurative* meaning of a metaphor of the form 'A is a φ' is the same as the *figurative* meaning of the counterpart simile of the form 'A is like a φ.'

This specification is incomplete since, as I have shown from classical sources, metaphors come in a variety of forms and transpose into similes in different ways, but these simple patterns will serve my present purposes.

The first thesis is that metaphors and similes literally say the same thing. The basic idea is that if one expression 'A' is elliptical for another expression 'B,' then 'A' has the same literal meaning as 'B.' Thus if metaphors are elliptical similes, then a metaphor must have the same meaning as its counterpart simile: the metaphorical utterance 'A is a φ' literally means that A is like a φ. In general, of course, sentences of the form 'A is a φ' do not have the same literal meaning as sentences of the form 'A is like a φ.' We tend to give sentences elliptical readings when this provides a natural way of preserving the truth or the relevance of what a speaker has said. With respect to truth, if someone refers to another as a jackal, it is usually more reasonable to suppose that the speaker is *comparing* that person with a jackal rather than lapsing into an inexplicable classificatory error. With respect to relevance, the fact that no man is an island is hardly a piece of information in need of dissemination, whereas the claim that no man is like an island is (or at least was) an arresting way of commenting on the human situation.[3]

3. This paragraph was occasioned by some searching criticisms from Ted Cohen. My defense of this first thesis would be stronger if I could give a general account of the conditions under which we give a sentence a

The second thesis is more important since it is this part of the traditional view that is most often misunderstood. A simile is not simply a literal comparison but is, instead, a figure of speech. That, I have suggested, is what Aristotle was getting at when he said that a simile is also a metaphor. *In particular, metaphors and similes both present figurative comparisons*. Since, however, they are both instances of figurative language, taken literally, the comparison must exhibit a (mutually recognized) incongruity, incompatibility, inappropriateness—no single word will do here—within the context in which the comparison is made. Figurative meaning arises, *in general*, through a (mutually recognized) mismatch of literal meaning with context, and, more specifically, this is how the figurativeness of figurative comparisons arises. *How* this happens will be the subject of close examination later on; here I am only insisting, as a second thesis, that the elliptical-simile theory of metaphor not only pairs the literal meaning of a metaphor with the literal meaning of the counterpart

---

reading as an ellipsis. I am not able to do this. The situation is complicated by the fact that two strategies seem to be available for dealing with the literal meaning of metaphorical utterances, and it is hard to think of decisive grounds for choosing between them. We can hold that 'Oskar is a jackal,' when used metaphorically, is *elliptical* for 'Oskar is like a jackal,' or we can say that, when used metaphorically, it is used to conversationally *imply* that Oskar is like a jackal.

I am inclined to favor the elliptical simile analysis because it seems to square with our tendency to speak of some metaphorical utterances as true. In this way metaphorical utterances seem different from ironic utterances where a conversational implication or an indirect speech act is typically generated by the perceived falsehood of the utterance.

More deeply, the fundamental themes of this work can be developed without choosing between these two ways of dealing with metaphorical utterances. As I shall argue in detail, critics of the traditional comparativist account of metaphors persistently misrepresent it as identifying the figurative meaning of a metaphor with the literal meaning of its counterpart simile. As Ted Cohen has pointed out to me, this argument relies on thesis II and is actually independent of thesis I.

simile, it also pairs the figurative meaning of a metaphor with the figurative meaning of the counterpart simile. Since metaphors and similes say the same things literally, their mismatch with context will give rise to the same figurative meaning. This, as a first approximation, is what the elliptical-simile or comparativist account of metaphors amounts to.[4]

4. In the closing chapter of this work I shall reformulate these theses in a way that eliminates the potentially misleading notion of *figurative meaning* in favor of the safer notion of *meaning something figuratively*. What that difference amounts to and why it is important can only be explained later.

4

The Standard Criticisms of Comparativism

Before developing the comparativist position in more detail, I shall examine, and attempt to answer, some of the standard criticisms that have been brought against it. These criticisms typically rest on two sorts of misrepresentations: (a) the basic structure of the position is misdescribed or (b) the position is gratuitously saddled with implausible doctrines foreign to it.

The standard misdescription of the comparativist position is that it identifies the *figurative* meaning of a metaphor with the *literal* meaning of its counterpart simile. Sometimes this interpretation is openly stated, but, often as not, it is simply taken for granted. As far as I know, this misreading of the comparativist position made its first appearance in Max Black's celebrated essay "Metaphor," and it has exercised a baleful influence since. I shall therefore deal with it first.

BLACK AGAINST THE COMPARATIVISTS

In cataloging various theories of metaphor, Black first introduces what he call the *substitution view of metaphor*, which, as he says, is "any view that holds that a metaphorical expression is used in place of some equivalent *literal* expression" (31). Here there seems to be a vague, half-remembered, echo of the view found in Aristotle, Cicero, and Quintilian, that in a metaphor a literal reference (for example, 'Achilles') is replaced by a metaphorical reference (for example, 'the lion'). But, according to these ancient writers, the point of this substitution is to produce a comparison, so we can simply move along to see what Black has to say against the comparativist account of metaphor.

> If a writer holds that a metaphor consists in the *presentation* of the underlying analogy or similarity, he will be taking what I shall call a *comparison view* of metaphor. . . . This is the view of metaphor as a condensed or elliptical *simile*. (35)

Fair enough! This, roughly, is the view I wish to defend. But Black continues the passage in a remarkable way:

> It will be noticed that a "comparison view" is a special case of a "substitution view." For it holds that the metaphorical statement might be replaced by an equivalent literal *comparison*. (35)

It is very hard to see how the view that treats "metaphor as a condensed or elliptical *simile*" has the consequence that "a metaphorical statement might be replaced by an equivalent literal comparison," unless Black is reasoning in the following way:

1. A metaphor is a condensed or elliptical simile.
2. Thus, except possibly for stylistic reasons, a metaphor can always be replaced by a simile.
3. Similes are statements of literal comparison.
4. Therefore, metaphorical statements can be replaced by equivalent literal comparisons.
5. But we cannot always find an adequate literal counterpart corresponding to the meaning of a metaphor.

6. Therefore, the first premise, that a metaphor is a condensed or elliptical simile, must be false.

But this is all wrong. In accepting the claim that a metaphor is a condensed or elliptical simile, the comparativist is not committed to step three of the argument; indeed, he rejects it. Not suffering from amnesia, the comparativist, unlike many of his critics, knows that similes, as figures of speech, present figurative, not literal comparisons. With a simile "one thing is likened to a *dissimilar* thing" (Lanham, 93). Thus the treatment of metaphors as elliptical similes is not a reduction of the figurative to the non-figurative; it is rather a specification of the kind of figurativeness metaphors possess. Metaphors are elliptical figurative *comparisons*.

As a variation on Black's argument, the comparativist might be charged with identifying the figurative meaning of a metaphor with some literal predication suggested by the comparison. On such a theory, the metaphorical utterance 'Richard is a lion' might just mean that Richard is brave. The comparativist, however, is not committed to identifying the figurative meaning of metaphors and similes with *any* such descriptive claims. In saying that one thing is like another, we are not *eo ipso* saying how.

Once we see that the comparativist is not committed to the doctrine that the figurative meaning of a metaphor always admits of replacement by a literal description, other common attacks on the position are easily turned. First, the comparativist is not committed to *producing* literal paraphrases of a metaphor and thus cannot be criticized for his failure to do so. Second, comparativism is not open to the charge that it reduces metaphors to mere stylistic embellishments. Here the critics' background reasoning seems to run as follows: "If metaphors could always be replaced by literal paraphrases which capture just what they mean, then the use of metaphors to convey such meaning would, strictly speaking, be unnecessary. Given this, metaphorical language could serve no other purpose but the merely decorative." First of all, it is unclear how the conclusion follows from the stated premises, and secondly the argument reveals a deep intellectualist prejudice against what is called the merely decorative. Ancient writers celebrated the power of metaphor to elevate both prose and poetry, whereas modern defenders of metaphor seem embarrassed by it. However this may be, the whole line of attack against comparativism is out of whack since comparativists are not committed to the literal reduction of metaphors attributed to them.

Furthermore, the comparativist need not be a chauvinist with respect to literal truth. He can hold that there is no clear boundary between literal and figurative language, and he can also hold that figurative language can achieve cognitive insight not possible with austerely literal language. He can, in fact, develop his position in a wide variety of frameworks without abandoning the comparativist position.

Yet we find critics of comparativism gratuitously freighting it with doctrines which are quite alien to the views of Aristotle, Cicero, and Quintilian. Mark Johnson, for example, associates comparativism with logical positivism apparently by means of the following train of free association: comparativism = the reduction of the metaphorical to the literal > literal truth chauvinism > logical positivism (Introduction, 16–19). Timothy Binkley first saddles the comparativists with the doctrine that "metaphorical claims are only disguised literal claims," and then proceeds to dilate at large on the subject in these words:

> According to this conception of the relationships among linguistic expressions and meanings, there are certain sentences we can really mean, and then there is that large class of sentences we do not really mean but which gallivant around wildly in even the most ordinary discourse as incognitos for the sentences which do express

"real" or "pure" meaning. We are presented with a picture of a realm where quintessential meanings subsist as demigods who can be directly approached only by the high priests of literal language: words represent meanings, only some words are on better terms with meanings than others. (145)

Binkley continues by saying "It is difficult to know how to react to this picture of language" (145). The real difficulty is to understand how this picture of language, or rather this parody of a picture of language, gets fastened onto the comparativist view of metaphors, particularly as it appeared in traditional sources.[1]

To summarize: A comparativist treats metaphors as elliptical similes and thereby identifies the literal and figurative meaning of the one, respectively, with the literal and figurative meaning of the other. In doing so, the comparativist:

1. Need not hold that the figurative meaning of a metaphor admits of an adequate literal translation;
2. Need not demote metaphors to mere stylistic embellishments; and
3. Need not adopt a narrow, cockamamie, theory of language.

A writer can be a comparativist concerning metaphors and *also* take up some of these additional positions. Perhaps some have, though I have found attempts to locate such views in ancient sources unconvincing.

In any case, in saying that I am committed to defending a comparativist view of metaphors, I am thus far only committed to the two theses presented at the beginning of this discussion. I am not committed to defending further theses that this or that comparativist may have held, and, most particularly, I wish to distance

1. Binkley's outburst is apparently triggered by some passages he cites from John Searle's *Speech Acts*. I have examined these passages and do not find anything in them like the picture of language that Binkley attacks.

myself as much as possible from various additional doctrines attributed to comparativism by critics whose primary intention is to make that position look bad.

SEARLE'S CRITICISMS OF COMPARATIVISM

Though many writers have been content to ring changes on Black's original attack on the comparativist view of metaphors, John Searle has, in his essay entitled "Metaphor," assembled a battery of arguments that do not, except, perhaps, in a few suspicious places, repeat Black's errors.

Searle offers three main arguments against comparativism. The first, as it seems to me, depends on assigning unnecessary referential baggage to comparativism. I shall dismiss it rather cavalierly. The other two arguments, on the other hand, present direct attacks on the comparativist view as I have characterized it, and, I believe, as it has been historically maintained. I do not think that either of these criticisms is correct, but they are searching criticisms that have the charm of relevance.

Searle says that "metaphorical meaning is always speaker's utterance meaning" ("Metaphor," 77). As we shall see, Searle means something stronger than this; he might better have expressed his view by saying that metaphorical meaning is *only* speaker's utterance meaning. But the remark introduces one of his key ideas, *speaker's utterance meaning*, and that needs explaining. Searle contrasts what he calls *speaker's utterance meaning* with what he calls *sentence* or *word* meaning:

> To have a brief way of distinguishing what a speaker means by uttering words, sentences, and expressions on the one hand, and what the words, sentences, and expressions mean on the other, I shall call the former *speaker's utterance meaning*, and the other *word*, or *sentence meaning*. (77)

According to Searle, speaker's utterance meaning can be related to sentence meaning in various ways. Where S is P represents the sentence meaning of what a person says and S is R represents the speaker's utterance meaning, we may distinguish various cases. I shall concentrate on three:

> *Literal Utterance.* A speaker says S is P and means S is P. Thus the speaker places the object S under the concept P, where $P = R$. Sentence meaning and utterance meaning coincide.
>
> *Ironic Utterance.* A speaker means the opposite of what he says. Utterance meaning is arrived at by going through the sentence meaning and then doubling back to the opposite of the sentence meaning.
>
> *Indirect Speech Act.* A speaker means what he says, but he means something more as well. The utterance meaning includes sentence meaning but extends beyond it. (115)

Now, it seems to me that there are two different distinctions at work in Searle's discussion: (1) whether the speaker intends his utterance to be taken literally or non-literally, and (2) whether the point (or at least the main point) of the utterance is exhausted in what is actually said. So we can distinguish literal from non-literal meaning and direct from indirect speech acts and get the following cross-classification:

	Literal	*Non-Literal*
Direct	Saying "The cat is on the mat," just meaning that the cat is on the mat.	Reciting nonsense poetry.
Indirect	Saying "This hike is longer than I remember," meaning (primarily) that I need a rest.	Saying "You're a real friend," meaning you're a louse.

Let me say a few words about each of these categories.

Literal/Direct   I think that we often intend our words to be taken quite literally, but it is probably fairly rare that we intend to convey no more information than what we actually state. (Only philosophers say that the cat is on the mat and let it go at that.) A la Grice, in standard conversational exchanges, our utterances carry with them a standard set of conversational implications generated by the rules that govern such exchanges.

Non-Literal/Direct   My first (wrong) instinct was that nothing could fall into this category, for if someone intentionally utters something without meaning it literally, then it would seem there must be something *else* he is literally trying to get across, else why produce an utterance at all? Nonsense poetry is a counter-example to this claim.

Literal/Indirect   In the given example, if the person who says that the hike is longer than he remembers expects his words to be taken literally, then whether the speech act is primarily direct or indirect will depend upon context. Bounding up the mountain in full fettle, the hikers might be reflecting on just how hard it is to remember past hikes, how long they were, and so forth. The remark would then be both literal and direct. If, however, we imagine the hikers exhausted, hauling themselves up a seemingly endless slope, then the speaker is probably trying to make the point that the hike has been long; long hikes are tiring; and so (indirectly) it is time for a breather.

Non-Literal/Indirect   I discussed utterances that fall into this category (primarily irony, hyperbole, and meiosis) in the previous chapter where I argued that with utterances of this kind the speaker expects the respondent to reject the actual utterance and replace it with another that corrects it or modifies it in certain ways. This stands in contrast with utterances that fall into the third category (the literal/indirect), where the speaker expects the respondent to *accept* the utterance, and then *add* something further.

Given this terminology, I think that the difference between Searle's view and that of the comparativists can be expressed this way: both Searle and the comparativists hold that the use of metaphors is an instance of an indirect speech act, that is, with metaphors we typically mean more than what we actually say and it is this "more" that really matters. Comparativists would, if asked, place metaphorical utterances in my third category: the utterance is intended literally (as a comparison), but the point is largely indirect. Searle, on the other hand, places metaphorical utterances in the fourth category: associating them with irony, he thinks that we do not intend our utterances to be taken literally. Who's right? In the end, the answer to this question will turn on a number of fine points, but before I reach these delicate issues, I have to deal with Searle's more heavy-handed way of treating them.

At first glance, it might seem that Searle is obviously right. If I say 'Sam is a pig,' it seems, on the assumption that Sam is a person, that I have said something that is literally false. In a context where the parties to the conversational exchange recognize this falsehood (and recognize that it is recognized, et cetera), the natural assumption is that this sentence was not intended to be taken literally. Searle provides a maxim for such occasions:

> Where the utterance is defective if taken literally, look
> for an utterance meaning that differs from the sentence
> meaning. (105)

Since, taken literally, it seems that virtually all metaphorical utterances are false, this maxim applies to them.

This, however, is not much of an argument and, in fact, Searle does not explicitly rely upon it. It is based on the curious idea that the literal meaning of an utterance is confined to the meanings of the words actually uttered. To see that this is wrong, consider the following exchange:

A: Are you coming?
B: In a little while.

I think that what this person literally said can be expressed this way:

B': (I'll come) in a little while.

As grammarians put it, the 'I'll come' is understood. Thus there would be nothing wrong in reporting B's speech act by saying that he said he was coming in a little while. Similarly, the comparativist says that the metaphorical utterance 'Sam is a pig' literally says the same thing as the simile 'Sam is like a pig.' The relevant respect in which Sam is said to be like a pig (for example, in behavior or appearance) will be fixed (more or less precisely) by context. This done, there would be nothing wrong with reporting the metaphorical speech act as follows: So-and-so thinks that Sam behaves like (or looks like) a pig.

With this argument from surface grammar out of the way, the easy interchangeability between metaphors and similes is so natural that it shifts the burden of proof to anyone who would deny that metaphors (like similes) make comparisons. Searle attempts to meet this burden of proof with a series of (at least) three arguments. I'll go through them one at a time.

1. Attacking what he calls crude versions of the comparison view, Searle says "that in the production and understanding of metaphorical utterances, there need not be any two objects for comparison" (87). The crude version of the comparativist theory that Searle has in mind must be something like this: the metaphor 'A is a B' is equivalent to the assertion that A exists, B exists, and A is similar to B. But this cannot be a correct account of metaphorical utterances, for, as Searle rightly points out, if I say that Sally is a block of ice, I am not saying that there exists

something that is a block of ice and Sally is similar to it. More pointedly, if I say that Sally is a dragon, I am not committing myself to the existence of (even one) dragon (87). Against such a crude theory, Searle concludes, quite correctly, that "it is just muddled about the referential character of expressions used metaphorically" (88).

I find this criticism completely out of focus. Whatever this or that comparativist may have said (perhaps unthinkingly), it is not an essential feature of the comparison view of metaphors that metaphors assert the existence of their objects of comparison. It is not essential since, often enough, *non*-figurative comparisons carry no such commitment. We can draw comparisons between existent and non-existent entities without, in stumblebum-fashion, inadvertently committing ourselves to the existence of something non-existent. The claim that Kissinger is more like Odysseus than Achilles does not carry with it a commitment to the historical existence of these two Greek figures. In sum, in holding that metaphors assert comparisons, the comparativist is not involved in referential muddles, since, so far at least, he has not committed his hand at all concerning reference. Of course, it is possible to combine a comparativist account of metaphors with a dumb account of comparative judgments themselves. This, in fact, is what Searle's crude version of the comparativist view amounts to.

2. Searle's second argument against the comparativist view of metaphors is that a metaphor cannot assert a comparison since a metaphor can be appropriate even when the (relevant) comparison is false.[2] He imagines someone remarking that Richard is a gorilla, meaning by this that Richard is "fierce, nasty, prone to violence, and so forth" (89). Now let's suppose, as is apparently true, that gorillas really aren't like that, but are, instead, "shy,

---

2. Monroe Beardsley presents essentially this same argument in his essay "The Metaphorical Twist" (294).

sensitive creatures, given to bouts of sentimentality" (89). So if someone says "Richard is a gorilla," meaning that Richard, who is fierce, nasty, prone to violence, and so forth, is similar to a gorilla, then what that person said would be false. On the other hand, if the speaker is not making a comparative judgment, then the remark, provided that Richard is fierce, nasty, prone to violence, and so forth, can be taken as true. So Searle concludes:

> My argument is starkly simple: in many cases the metaphorical statement and the corresponding similarity statement cannot be equivalent in meaning because they have different truth conditions. (90)

The first thing to say about this argument is that it relies upon a metaphor that is quite dead. On Searle's own account, with dead metaphors, the literal meaning is bypassed, and what previously was a metaphorical meaning has become a new literal meaning. So, as a dead metaphor, the truth condition for "Richard is a gorilla" is just that he is fierce, nasty, prone to violence, and so forth. Through repetition, the metaphor ceases to be a metaphor and becomes an instance of the category of direct and literal meaning.

A more subtle case lies nearby. Suppose A and B are primate anthropologists. They both know that gorillas are shy, sensitive creatures, et cetera. Now suppose, over drinks, A describes someone as a gorilla; how will B respond to him? That's hard to say. He might remark that it's unfair (to gorillas). He might also respond to it as a dead metaphor. Finally, and this is the subtle case, he might respond to it as representing the common view (though not the speaker's view) concerning gorillas. He is responding to a claim that could be paraphrased as follows:

> Richard is like what (most people think) a gorilla is like.

There are actually two ways that we might treat this case. First, we can say that the person is saying that Richard is like what most people think gorillas are like, and has simply dropped the qualifying reference to most people's beliefs. This is the way of ellipsis. In this case, everything said is literally said, but not everything literally claimed is put into words. Alternatively, we can say that the person draws the comparison from an assumed perspective. Here he speaks from the perspective of common belief which he and his listener know contains false beliefs they do not share. We might call them assumed-perspective statements and, as such, they are close to comparisons made between actual and fictitious beings. Such cross-comparisons, however, are not embarrassing to the comparativist.[3]

3. Under the title "A Further Examination of the Comparison Theory," Searle presents a more interesting line of criticism.

> Yet another objection is this: It is crucial to the simile thesis [as Searle now calls it] that the simile be taken literally; yet there seem to be a great many metaphorical utterances where there is no relevant literal corresponding similarity between S and P. (95)

3. In discussing the gorilla example, Searle makes one of his few remarks about similes:

Similar remarks apply incidentally to similes. If I say,

(16) Sam acts like a gorilla

that need not commit me to the truth of

(17) Gorillas are such that their behavior resembles Sam's.

For (16) need not be about gorillas at all, and we might say that "gorilla" in (16) has a metaphorical occurrence. ("Metaphor," 91–92)

The remarks that I have made concerning metaphors apply here as well. In this same context, Searle lapses into pleonasm when he distinguishes *figurative* similes from literal statements of similarity. This is Searle's closest encounter with the comparativist theory of the traditional kind.

Taking the specimen "Sally is a block of ice," he tells us:

> There simply is no class of predicates, R, such that Sally
> is literally like a block of ice with respect to R where R is
> what we intended to predicate of Sally when we said she
> was a block of ice. (96)

The obvious response is that both Sally and blocks of ice are cold.
Searle anticipates this response:

> Temperature metaphors for emotional and personal traits
> are in fact quite common and they are not derived from
> any literal underlying similarities. Thus we speak of a
> "heated argument," "a warm welcome," "a lukewarm
> friendship," and "sexual frigidity." Such metaphors are
> fatal for the simile thesis, unless the defenders can
> produce a literal R which S and P have in common, and
> which is sufficient to explain the precise metaphorical
> meaning which is conveyed. (98)

Let's spell this argument out in detail. A suppressed underlying premise seems to be something like this:

1. If S is similar to P, then there must be some specifiable
   feature R such that both of them literally possess it.

Notice that this is a thesis about similarity claims in general, and
not just about metaphorical statements and similes. Now, according to Searle:

2. There are some metaphors and similes where no such
   feature R can be found which (a) both S and P share and
   which (b) provides the basis for the metaphor.

He then concludes that metaphors are not assertions of similarity.

Now it seems to me that the first premise of this argument is
just false; and I'm not the first person to see and say this. In the
appendix to the *Treatise* Hume remarks:

> Tis evident, that even different simple ideas may have a
> similarity or resemblance to each other; nor is it neces-
> sary, that the point or circumstance of the resemblance
> shou'd be distinct or separable from that in which they
> differ. Blue and green are different simple ideas, but are
> more resembling than blue and scarlet; though their
> perfect simplicity excludes all possibility of separation or
> distinction. (*Treatise* 637)

Unfortunately, Hume expresses himself in terms of his distinction
between simple and complex ideas—a distinction that melts
under scrutiny—but surely the point he is making is correct: two
different shades of blue, for example, resemble each other without there being any common distinguishable feature in virtue of
which they resemble each other. Of course, they resemble each
other in being different shades of *blue,* but this is what distinguishes them as well, that is, that they are *different* shades of
blue. Thus, Searle's argument seems to rely on the principle that
for one thing to be similar to another there must be some feature
that they (non-trivially) share. That principle seems to be false.

In order to explore this issue further, let me introduce the
notion of a brute similarity. I shall say that a similarity is brute if
there is no independently identifiable feature, F, such that the
similarity is (non-trivially) based upon sharing this feature. I'm
not sure that the notion of a brute similarity will stand up to close
examination, but I introduce it only to formulate a response to my
criticism of Searle's argument. Someone, perhaps Searle, might
argue in the following way: the similarity between two shades of
blue may be brute, but the metaphor involved in calling Sally a
block of ice cannot be based upon even a brute similarity because
the comparison, if it exists, would be cross-categorical.

But cross-category brute similarities do seem to occur. We
can say, for example, that things from different categories are
simple. Mathematical proofs, recipes, designs, the way to a
friend's house, the instructions for assembling a lawn chair, can

all be simple. More to the point, certain colors and sounds seem hot, others cold or cool. Here Searle might respond that these temperature attributions to colors and sounds are themselves metaphorical. But why say that? The only reason that I can see is an acceptance of the principle that for one thing to resemble another, there must be some independent feature which they both non-trivially share. That principle is plainly false for many intra-categorical comparisons where brute similarities (for example, between colors) plainly exist, and it doesn't seem obviously true that there are no brute cross-categorical comparisons. In sum, Searle's third argument against the comparativist account of metaphors depends upon an unstated (hence undefended) account of similarity that we are not constrained to accept.

It seems to me that I have surveyed all of Searle's arguments against the comparativist view of metaphors and none of them seems to override the presumption that metaphors, like similes, put forward comparisons, albeit figurative comparisons.

THE GOODMAN AND DAVIDSON ATTACKS ON COMPARATIVISM

Searle's attack upon comparativism depended, in part at least, on a view concerning the nature of similarity claims, namely, that for one thing to be like another they must share an independently identifiable significant feature. Here, I shall examine two further attacks upon comparativism that also turn upon special views concerning similarity claims. The first is found in Nelson Goodman's "Seven Strictures on Similarity"; the second comes from Donald Davidson's "What Metaphors Mean."

Goodman

In his splendid essay, "Seven Strictures on Similarity," Nelson Goodman submits that similarity is insidious. More fully:

> Similarity, ever ready to solve philosophical problems
> and overcome obstacles, is a pretender, an imposter, a
> quack. *It has, indeed, its place and its uses,* but is more
> often found where it does not belong, professing powers it
> does not possess. (Emphasis added, 437)

As the italicized passage indicates, Goodman is not proscribing
all appeals to similarity, a point he had already insisted upon in
Languages of Art:

> Neither here nor elsewhere have I argued that there is no
> constant relation of resemblance; judgments of similarity
> in selected and familiar respects are, even though rough
> and fallible, as objective and categorical as any that are
> made in describing the world. (39*n*)

Appeals to similarity become insidious when they are not modest-
ly restricted to "selected and familiar respects," and when they
are not controlled, in Goodman's words, by "conceptual and
perceptual habit" and embedded in "representational custom."
Philosophers (theoreticians), however, often use similarity claims
in the absence of these necessary constraints. They are the target
of Goodman's seven strictures.

In his *first stricture,* for example, Goodman tells us that
similarity does not "account for the grading of pictures as more or
less realistic or naturalistic" (437).[4] In the first place, "we must
beware of supposing that similarity constitutes any firm, invariant
criterion of realism; for similarity is relative, variable, culture
dependent" (438). Secondly, reversing the direction of explanation, he points out that our involvement in our culture's customary
modes of representation may influence what strikes us as being
similar or resembling. In *Languages of Art* he makes the point this
way:

4. The central themes of the first stricture are presented in the first
chapter of Goodman's *Languages of Art*.

Representational customs, which govern realism, also tend to generate resemblance. (39)

Following a similar pattern, in the *fifth stricture* Goodman tells us that:

Similarity does not account for our predictive, or more generally, our inductive practice. (441)

The reason is that "no matter what happens, the future will be in some way like the past" (441) and therefore

our predictions cannot be based upon the bald principle that the future will resemble the past. The question is *how* what is predicted is like what has already been found. Along which among countless lines of similarities do our predictions run? I suspect that rather than similarity providing any guidelines for inductive practice, inductive practice may provide the basis for some canons of similarity. (441)

Once more we have a double move: first, a rejection of the explanatory force of a *bald* appeal to similarity; second, a suggestion that explanation may, in part at least, run in the reverse direction.[5]

Goodman's *fourth stricture*, which is our present concern, says:

Similarity does not explain metaphor or metaphorical truth. (440)

Why? Goodman's answer falls into the familiar pattern. First, bald appeals to similarity are unconstrained and thus lack explanatory power:

to proclaim that certain tones are soft because they are like soft materials, or blue because they are like colors,

---

5. The *locus classicus* for Goodman's views on induction is *Fact, Fiction, and Forecast*, in particular, chaps. 3 and 4 (in the fourth edition).

explains nothing. Anything is in some ways like anything
else . . . (440)

Then, once more, he suggests that we might do better to treat
similarity as an explanandum rather than the explanans:

Metaphorical use may serve to explain the similarity
better than—or at least as well as—the similarity explains the metaphor. (440)

To begin with, let me say that I think that Goodman is surely
right in his first point: bald appeals to similarity typically lack the
explanatory power that philosophers are apt to attribute to them. I
think he may also be right in saying that similarity might better be
explained by various phenomena that it is sometimes presented
as explaining. More carefully, and Goodman's phrasing suggests
this, our notions of similarity and representation, similarity and
inductive practice, similarity and metaphorical use are respectively intertwined and mutually supportive. In each case similarity demands explanation *together with* its companion.

How do these considerations bear upon the traditional comparativist account of metaphors? In what I take to be an allusion to
the traditional position, Goodman remarks:

Metaphor is . . . construed as elliptical simile, and
metaphorical truths as elliptical literal truths. (440)

While the first part of this sentence is perfectly correct, the
second, as I have said repeatedly, completely misrepresents the
comparativist position. Metaphorical truths, if we want to use this
expression, are elliptical *figurative* (not literal) truths.

This response to Goodman is too quick, for even if he
misdescribes the target of his criticism, isn't it still true that the
comparativist, in his explanation of metaphors, makes just the
kind of bald appeal to similarity that Goodman rejects? The
answer to this is no. The comparativist identifies the literal and
figurative meaning of a metaphor respectively with the literal and

figurative meaning of a counterpart simile. Concentrating on the counterpart simile for a moment, two things are worth saying: (i) similes, as they occur in daily life, in poetry, et cetera, are typically specific, determinate, and not bald assertions of resemblance of the kind that Goodman rejects; and (ii) similes (to say it again) are figurative comparisons gaining their indirect content in virtue of an incongruency (of one sort or another) with the determinate context in which they occur. Thus treating metaphors as elliptical similes has none of the bad consequences that Goodman envisages. It does not identify metaphors with (or reduce them to) empty similarity claims; it treats them as elliptical similes.

Davidson

Part of the difficulty with understanding Davidson's essay "What Metaphors Mean" is that it is motivated, at least in part, by a background theory that is not explicitly stated. It is, however, alluded to a number of times, as in the following passage:

> Literal meaning and literal truth conditions can be assigned to words and sentences apart from particular context of use. This is why adverting to them has genuine explanatory value. (33)

This passage falls so casually from Davidson's pen that the general reader might take it to be a commonplace. In fact, it invokes a complex and highly controversial position that Davidson and his followers have been developing over the past few decades. The leading idea is that a theory of meaning for a natural language consists of giving truth conditions for the sentences of that language.[6]

---

6. The primitive insight is that the meaning of a sentence is given by those conditions which make it true. Since, however, the speaker of a

The passage can also be misread. It may sound as if Davidson is saying that the literal meaning and literal truth conditions of a sentence are independent of context, but this is not what he means. For Davidson, the literal truth conditions (and presumably the literal meaning[7]) of a sentence containing indexicals (for example, 'This was left here yesterday') will depend upon the context in which the sentence is uttered. Davidson's point is that the literal meaning of a sentence is not affected by the *use* to which it is put. A person might use the sentence 'The cat is on the mat' to achieve various purposes: to tell someone where the cat is, to tell someone what a mat (or cat) is, or, more remotely, to demonstrate a command of the English language, but whatever the point of making the remark might be, the sentence 'The cat is on the mat' is true if and only if the cat is, after all, on the mat. Thus Davidson is not saying that meaning and truth are independent of context, but rather, that meaning and truth are independent of the context of *use*. "I depend," he tells us, "on [this] distinction between what words mean and what they are used to do" (33).

With this background, I turn to Davidson's leading thesis that "metaphors mean what the words, in their most literal interpretation, mean, and nothing more" (32). According to Davidson, if someone says, metaphorically, that Harold is a pig, then he is literally asserting that Harold is a *pig*. His sentence does not *mean* anything more than this. Of course, in common parlance,

language can produce an unlimited number of sentences with novel meanings, the specification of these truth conditions must be done in a systematic (typically recursive) way. The technical details of this program are complex and will not be pursued here. Fortunately, there is no need to do so since, as we shall see, Davidson's central criticism of the comparativist account of metaphors turns upon a particular thesis concerning likeness or resemblance claims, namely, that they are, one and all, true.

7. At one place Davidson speaks of "what a sentence literally means (given its context)" (44).

we might say that the *person* who used this sentence meant to indicate that Harold is, say, a sloppy eater. Even so, and here let me say at once that I think that Davidson is absolutely right, this does not alter the meaning of the sentence uttered.

But if the person is literally saying (or saying literally) that Harold is a pig, then what he says is false and this, in general, is how it is with metaphors:

> If a sentence used metaphorically is true or false in the ordinary sense, then it is clear that it is usually false. (41)[8]

Finally, what, according to Davidson, is the point of uttering such falsehoods which, unlike lies, are uttered with the intention that the falsehood be recognized? He answers this question in a variety of ways:

> A metaphor *makes* [emphasis added] us attend to some likeness, often a novel or surprising likeness, between two or more things. (33)
> . . . when "mouth" applied only metaphorically to bottles, the application *made* [emphasis added] the hearer *notice* [his emphasis] a likeness between animal and bottle openings. (37)
> . . . a simile tells us, in part, what a metaphor *nudges* [emphasis added] us into noting. (38)

---

8. I'm not sure how the qualifying clause "If a sentence used metaphorically is true or false in the ordinary sense," is intended. One possibility is that it acknowledges the existence of metaphorical expressions in sentences that are not true or false, for example, in questions and imperatives. A provision should be made for such occurrences. More plausibly, as Ted Cohen suggests, the qualification leaves open the possibility that even metaphorical sentences in the indicative lack a truth value. This fits the line of Davidson's argument that the meaning of a metaphorical sentence must be its literal meaning at the pain of its having no meaning at all.

So, strictly speaking, a sentence has no metaphorical meaning; its meaning is just its direct flat-footed literal meaning. On the other hand, in using a sentence metaphorically we typically employ a patent falsehood in order to make our listener notice, or nudge him into noticing, a similarity (often novel or surprising) between the things spoken of in the false utterance. In sum, Davidson has given us a causal theory of what others have called metaphorical meaning. At least he has sketched the outlines of such a theory.

Davidson's causal theory is, I believe, in some ways original, but in one respect he falls in step with other recent writers on metaphor: in developing his own position, he feels called upon to reject the traditional comparativist theory of metaphors. At first glance it may seem that Davidson's leading thesis, that "metaphors mean what the words, in their most literal interpretation, mean, and nothing more" (32), is clearly incompatible with traditional comparativism. But, as Davidson himself sees, this is quite wrong. A person who holds the elliptical-simile theory of metaphors maintains that the metaphorical sentence 'Harold is a pig' *literally* means the same thing as 'Harold is like a pig.' In criticizing Black's interpretation of the comparativist view, Davidson puts this just right:

> if metaphors are elliptical similes, they say *explicitly* what similes say, for ellipsis is a form of abbreviation, not of paraphrase or indirection. (39)

It strikes me as a bit odd to say that an elliptical expression says *explicitly* the same thing that its non-elliptical counterpart says, but in any case, it does *literally* say the same thing. It then follows that there is no reason why Davidson, given his leading thesis, could not accept the elliptical-simile account of metaphors. But he does not. I will now examine why.

Davidson distinguishes two versions of the comparativist view of metaphors. The first, which, for reasons that escape me, he calls the more "sophisticated variant," tells us that "the figurative meaning of a metaphor is the literal meaning of the corresponding simile" (38).[9] This, as I have argued, is the worst way of interpreting the comparativist account of metaphors. Davidson then goes on to distinguish it from "the common theory that a metaphor is an elliptical simile" (38). Having gotten this much right, he then goes on to offer the following curious criticism of this second version of the comparativist view.

> This theory makes no distinction in meaning between a metaphor and some related simile and does not provide any ground for speaking of figurative, metaphorical, or special meanings. (38–39)

I'm not sure what Davidson is getting at here, but perhaps it comes to this: anyone who identifies the meaning of a metaphor with the meaning of a counterpart simile, *and then goes his way*, has hardly produced a theory of the figurative meaning of metaphors. (In contrast, the person who presents the more 'sophisticated variant' of the comparativist position, by identifying the figurative meaning of a metaphor with the literal meaning of the counterpart simile, has at least produced a theory, albeit a very bad one.) The obvious rejoinder is that the person who recommends an elliptical-simile account of metaphorical meaning is not constrained to stop there. The theory amounts to treating both metaphors and similes as figurative comparisons. The next step, which will be pursued in the following chapters, is to explain how figurative comparisons function.

Davidson's second complaint against treating metaphors as elliptical similes goes as follows:

9. This is reminiscent of Nelson Goodman's characterization of the comparativists in these words: "Metaphor is thus construed as elliptical simile, and metaphorical truths as elliptical literal truths" ("Strictures," 440).

> if we make the literal meaning of the metaphor to be the literal meaning of a matching simile, we deny access to what we originally took to be the literal meaning of the metaphor, and we agreed almost from the start that *this* meaning was essential to the working of the metaphor. (39)

This is surely odd, for how can *identifying* the meaning of 'a' with 'b' *deny access* to the meaning of 'a'? Only, I suppose, if we thought (or agreed) that we knew the meaning of 'a' and then went on to identify it with something 'b' whose meaning is in doubt. Nothing like that, however, is going on in the elliptical-simile theory of metaphors. The *literal* meaning of a counterpart simile is transparent; it is just the claim that *a* is like *b*. In fact, it is hard not to think that Davidson hasn't repeated Black's mistake, except in reverse form. Black identified the figurative meaning of a metaphor with the literal meaning of the counterpart simile, then complained that figurativeness was lost. Davidson identifies the literal meaning of a metaphor with the figurative meaning of the counterpart simile and then complains that the literal meaning of the metaphorical expression is lost. Schematically, the situation looks like this:

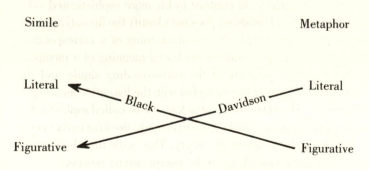

The suspicion that Davidson, despite clear texts that show he knows better, is lapsing back into mistaken criticisms reminiscent of Black, is further borne out by the following passage:

> Both the elliptical simile theory of metaphor and its more sophisticated variant, which equates the figurative meaning of the metaphor with the literal meaning of a simile, share a fatal defect. They make the hidden meaning of the metaphor all too obvious and accessible. In each case the hidden meaning is to be found simply by looking to the literal meaning of what is usually a painfully trivial simile. This is like that—Tolstoy is like an infant, the earth like a floor. It is trivial because everything is like everything else. Metaphors are often very difficult to interpret and, so it is said, impossible to paraphrase. But with this theory, interpretation and paraphrase typically are ready to the hand to the most callow. (39)

This passage contains two criticisms, both wrong, but it will take some work sorting them out. The first is that comparativism, in either form, makes the hidden meaning of a metaphor too easy to interpret; the second is that hidden meaning, when revealed, usually emerges as triviality. To say it one final time, the traditional comparativist, in contrast to his more sophisticated sidekick invented by Davidson, does not identify the figurative meaning of a metaphor with the literal meaning of a corresponding simile; instead, he identifies the literal meaning of a metaphor with the literal meaning of the corresponding simile and the figurative meaning of the metaphor with the figurative meaning of that simile. Thus Davidson's attack on the so-called sophisticated theory of metaphor, which is sound enough, does not carry over to the normal (elliptical-simile) theory. This is the first thing wrong with Davidson's attack upon the comparativist position.

In his second criticism, Davidson claims that comparativism, in either of the forms he distinguishes, identifies the 'hidden' meaning of a metaphor with "what is usually a painfully trivial simile." Later he elaborates on this claim in these words:

> The most obvious semantic difference between simile and metaphor is that all similes are true and most metaphors are false. The earth is like a floor, the Assyrian did come down like a wolf on the fold, because *everything is like everything*. (Emphasis added, 41)[10]

I think that Davidson's intentions here are clear: all similes are true because all comparative statements, including those we would not naturally call similes, are true. They are all true because everything is like everything. Thus reducing metaphors to similes has the result that metaphors, like similes, are always boringly true.

Why should Davidson hold that everything is like everything? I suspect that it follows from a commitment to two more primitive theses:

D1. Two things are similar if there is at least one thing that is true of both.

D2. Given any two things, it is always possible to find something (indeed, endlessly many things) true of both.

Taken together, these theses clearly imply that everything is like everything.

The first instinct of those unfamiliar with these matters is to challenge D2. It may seem implausible that given *any* two things, we can always find something (not to say endlessly many things) true of both of them. In fact, once we see how little D2 is saying, it becomes clear that it is obviously, trivially, true. For example,

---

10. Notice that Davidson's claim that everything is like everything is stronger than Goodman's remark that "anything is in some way like anything else . . ." ("Strictures" 440). Goodman seems to hold that philosophers' similarity claims are sometimes empty truths lacking explanatory power. He does not hold that this is true of all similarity claims.

the Washington Monument and the fourth root of seven have endlessly many things in common since they share properties of the following kind:

That of being identical with the Washington Monument, or with the fourth root of seven, or with the number one.

Using this pattern as our guide, one can churn out shared properties *ad libidum*.[11]

It may seem that we can avoid the result that everything is like everything simply by specifying a *respect* in which the likeness claim is made. There are, however, a number of theoretical problems that may preclude the completion of such a project. In particular, it could be argued that limitation by respects is no limitation at all, because everything is like everything in *every* respect. The argument to show this will depend again upon the construction of curious artificial predicates. Suppose that the claim is made that a is not like b in respect ϕ, for example, that deGaulle was not like Churchill in respect to height.

1. Find any two properties that the two entities share, for example, being governed by the law of identity.
2. Disjoin this property with the property specifying the respect in which the comparison is being made, yielding, for example, the property of being either taller than average height or governed by the law of identity.

This is a property, respecting height, that both entities share, so deGaulle is similar to Churchill with respect to height after all.

Here someone might respond that this weird disjunctive property does not concern height, though it is hard to see how that

---

11. They have non-denumerably many things in common because we can substitute any real number for the number one.

argument might go. [12] More directly, it could be said that this disjunctive property is perfectly stupid—altogether useless. This, I think, is the right thing to say, but such an appeal to *pragmatics* (as it is called) is not countenanced by the austere theory of meaning and truth favored by Davidson. Finally, we might try to tighten down the respect by identifying it with a *specific* property. We might say that deGaulle differed from Churchill in the following respect: deGaulle was over six feet tall, whereas Churchill was not. Now, however, the reference to similarity seems to have evaporated, for all we are saying is that deGaulle was over six feet tall and Churchill was not. Indeed, it now seems that we can give up the idea that similarity claims serve any indispensable cognitive purpose, for where we formerly said that a is similar to b but not to c in respect ϕ, we can now say instead that a has some feature ϕ, so does b, but not c. It seems that we can abandon the practice of making similarity claims altogether. [13]

I have dwelled on these matters because it is important to see that the Davidson view of metaphor (and, in particular, his dismissal of the comparativist approach) is driven by his special views concerning similarity claims. For him, all similarity claims

12. To gain an appreciation of the theoretical difficulties raised by such arbitrary constructions, see Nelson Goodman, "The New Riddle of Induction," in *Fact, Fiction, and Forecast*, and A. N. Prior, "The Autonomy of Ethics."

13. I think that this is the point that Nelson Goodman is making when he says:

> But when to the statement that two things are similar we add a specification of the property they have in common, we . . . remove an ambiguity; but rather than supplementing our initial statement, we render it superfluous. For as we have already seen, to say two things are similar in having a specified property in common is to say nothing more than that they have that property in common ("Strictures," 444–45).

are literally true because everything is similar to everything. In his *Philosophical Commentaries*, Berkeley declared that in all things he agreed with the mob. My commitment to the opinions of the mob are not so broad as Berkeley's, but I certainly think that the mob is right, contra Davidson, in thinking that some similarity claims are true and others false. I do not deny (D2), that, given any two entities (existent, non-existent, or mixed), it is always possible to find something that is true of both; I deny (D1), that this shows that they are similar. To establish this, I shall challenge a seemingly safer view, namely, that if a is similar to b, then b must be similar to a. Over against the claim that similarity is a *universal*[14] relation (that is, a relation that holds between all entities), I shall argue that it is not even a *symmetrical* relation. Of course, if similarity is a universal relation, it follows trivially that it is a symmetrical relation; thus by showing that similarity is not symmetrical we refute the doctrine that everything is similar to everything else. This in turn forces us to reject (D1), the claim that two things are similar if at least one thing is true of both.

REVERSIBILITY

My attention was first drawn to the matter of the symmetry of similarity claims by Monroe C. Beardsley's fine essay "The Metaphorical Twist." There he produces an ingenious criticism of the comparativist account of metaphors. He first maintains that "a statement of likeness is equivalent to its own converse" (297), that is, likeness statements are symmetrical: if a is like (similar to) b, then b is like (similar to) a. But metaphors are not always (or even often) reversible in this way. Citing an example from R. P. Blackmur, he points out, quite correctly, that "this man is a lion" seems radically different in meaning from "this lion is a man." To

14. Goodman's phrase is "universal and hence useless" relation ("Strictures" 443).

give another example, "no man is an island" seems wholly different in significance from "no island is a man." The argument, then, comes to this: since similarity statements are symmetrical and metaphorical statements are not, metaphorical statements are not statements of similarity.

Actually, as stated, this argument draws too strong a conclusion. There might be metaphors that are symmetrical (reversible) and these metaphors, at least, might express similarity claims. I shall not, however, press this point, since I have a deeper criticism of the *reversibility argument,* as I shall now call it. The underlying assumption of the reversibility argument is that non-figurative similarity claims are symmetrical. I shall argue that this assumption is false.

To start with a personal experience, I was once struck by the present pope's likeness (in a photograph) to Arnold Palmer. It was not difficult to identify the source of this likeness: the pope has Arnold Palmer's eyes. At the same time, I felt no compulsion to say that Arnold Palmer looked like the pope. Why not? The answer, I think, is that Arnold Palmer's eyes—that crinkled down-the-fairway squint—are one of the distinctive features of his face: it would appear, for example, in caricatures drawn of him. On the other hand, Arnold Palmer eyes are not distinctive features of the pope's face. Put very crudely, it seemed to me that the pope resembled Arnold Palmer, but not conversely, because the pope possessed one of Arnold Palmer's distinctive features whereas Arnold Palmer did not possess a distinctive feature of the pope. To cite another example, and they are easily multiplied, beach chairs look like clothespins (the kind with springs), but clothespins do not look like beach chairs.[15]

15. This example comes from Florence Fogelin. Gombrich makes a similar point about likenesses in appearance by comparing a photograph taken of Bertrand Russell when he was four years old with one taken when he was ninety years old. "Those who are familiar with Bertrand Russell's striking features will inevitably . . . try to find the old man in the young

Where I have spoken of *distinctive features*, cognitive psychologists speak of *salience*. In his seminal paper, "Features of Similarity," Amos Tversky states the matter this way:

> Similarity judgments can be regarded as extensions of similarity statements, that is, statements of the form "a is like b." Such a statement is directional; it has a subject, a, and a referent, b, and it is not equivalent in general to the converse similarity statement "b is like a." In fact, a choice of subject and referent depends, at least in part, on the relative salience of the objects. We tend to select the more salient stimulus, or the prototype, as a referent, and the less salient stimulus, or variant, as a subject. We say "the portrait resembles the person" rather than "the person resembles the portrait." We say "the son resembles the father" rather than "the father resembles the son." We say "an ellipse is like a circle," not "a circle is like an ellipse," and we say "North Korea is like Red China" rather than "Red China is like North Korea." (328)

This passage contains two components: (i) a list of clear examples of non-figurative similarity claims that are not reversible and (ii) a general claim, in terms of *salience*, intended to explain this phenomenon. It is important to see that the first point *alone* is sufficient to refute Beardsley's claim that metaphors are not similarity claims because similarity claims are symmetrical and metaphors (often) are not. And *a fortiori*, it refutes Davidson's claim that everything is, after all, similar to everything else.

It may be true that reversing metaphors and similes (typically)

---

child; his mother, if she could be alive, would look in the features of the old man for traces of the child" (7). There is no need for the striking features of the child to be the same as the striking features of the old man, and in such a case, for example, the four-year-old Russell might look like the ninety-year-old Russell, but not conversely. [This passage from Gombrich was pointed out to me by Ted Cohen.]

produces more strikingly incongruous results. Tversky suggests this:

> The directionality and asymmetry of similarity relations are particularly noticeable in similes and metaphors. We say that "Turks fight like tigers" and not "tigers fight like Turks." (328)[16]

It might be interesting to know why (if it is true) metaphors and similes have reversals that tend to be more incongruous than the reversals of non-figurative comparisons. [17] Nonetheless, the phenomenon of incongruous reversal cannot be used to distinguish similes and metaphors from non-figurative comparisons, since the phenomenon is exhibited by them all.

With salience, the concept that Tversky uses to explain the phenomenon of incongruous reversal, the philosophical instinct is to ask for an analysis or definition of this key notion. In fact, Tversky says little that satisfies this demand. He provides a number of examples of incongruous reversals, but this is a mixed bag where irreversibility arises for different reasons. Consider the appeal to *prototypes*. Prototypes are typically *set up* to be imitated, and it is therefore not surprising that saying a prototype resembles one of its echo-types will sound peculiar. [18] The irreversibility of "an ellipse is like a circle" seems to have a wholly different source, and later, Tversky explains it this way:

> A major determinant of salience of geometric figures is goodness of form. Thus, a "good figure" is likely to be more salient than a "bad figure." (334)

16. Notice that Tversky here takes for granted the traditional view that similes and metaphors express similarities.

17. One possible answer is that metaphors start out with a base of incongruity that can be built upon.

18. Although it may seem odd to say that a face serves as a prototype for a portrait, the relationship between prototype/copy and subject/portrait is close. In both cases, the first member of the pair sets the standard for the second.

The irreversibility of "North Korea is like Red China" seems to derive from yet other sources, though a further specification of context would be needed to spell this out. It seems, then, that salience can arise for a variety of heterogeneous reasons that may defy any reduction to a simple theory. This comes out in Tversky's most general characterization of salience:

> The salience . . . of a feature is determined by two types of factors: intensive and diagnostic. The former refers to factors that increase intensity or signal-to-noise ratio, such as the brightness of a light, the loudness of a tone, the saturation of a color, the size of a letter, the frequency of an item, the clarity of a picture, or the vividness of an image. The diagnostic factors refer to the classificatory significance of features, that is, the importance or prevalence of the classifications that are based on these features. (342)

Roughly, features are salient in the first way when they stand out, are prominent or conspicuous. Features are salient in the second way when they play a central role in classifying or sorting things out. In bird identification, eye rings (split or unsplit) and wing bars are sometimes salient features in this second way, but, as every birder knows, they are often not salient in the first way.

Salience, then, is a rich and diverse concept—perhaps in need of regimentation. Salience is also highly context-bound, a point also stressed by Tversky.

> Like other judgments, similarity depends on context and frame of reference. Sometimes the relevant frame of reference is specified explicitly, as in the questions, "How similar are English and French with respect to sound?" "What is the similarity of a pear and an apple with respect to taste?" In general, however, the relevant feature space is not specified explicitly but rather inferred from the general context. (340)

But even if the feature space is not always specified explicitly, judgments of similarity always take place within a space where certain features make themselves count (type one salience) or are made to count (type two salience). Because of the contextual constraints imposed by a delimiting feature space, not all claims to similarity are alike in being boringly true.

I can now draw some negative conclusions. First, metaphors cannot be distinguished from literal similarity claims, as Beardsley thought, by an appeal to the phenomenon of incongruous reversal. Second, metaphors cannot be distinguished from literal similarity claims, as Merrie Bergmann seems to suggest, by an appeal to salience. Here is what she says:

> What is distinctive of all metaphorical uses of language (whether the purpose is to assert or to do something else) is that the content of what is communicated is a *direct* function of salient characteristics associated with (at least) part of the expression—rather than of the literal meaning of that part. (234)

If Tversky is right—and he only has to be *generally* right, and not right in *detail*—then this feature that Bergmann finds distinctive of metaphors is a common feature of all comparisons, both figurative and non-figurative.

Finally, I return to Davidson's criticisms that started these reflections on similarity and note that the comparativist does not make "the hidden meaning of a metaphor all too obvious and accessible" by identifying it with "the literal meaning of what is usually a painfully trivial simile" (38). This is doubly wrong. The comparativist does not identify the hidden (I would prefer to say the *figurative*) meaning with the literal meaning of a simile; that's Black's old mistake. Nor is there any reason to suppose that the associated simile is "usually[19] painfully trivial"; that's Davidson's new mistake.

19. On his own account, Davidson should have said "*always* painfully trivial."

5

A Dilemma for Theories of Metaphor

In the previous chapter I tried to rescue the comparativist view of metaphors from beneath the avalanche of criticism under which it has been buried. In this chapter I shall look at some of the alternative theories that have been offered in its place. I shall argue that theories of metaphor must solve a basic dilemma concerning metaphorical truth, and further argue that, as far as I can see, the comparativist view alone is able to solve this dilemma in a natural way.

One question that a theory of metaphor should answer is what, after all, is being said when someone produces a metaphorical utterance? For example, one version of the substitution view, which may only exist as a target of criticism, is that the metaphorical utterance 'John is a lion' just means that John is brave. [1] I shall classify this as a *meaning-shift* theory of metaphor, including

---

1. A more sophisticated *cluster* theory might identify the meaning of the claim that John is a lion with the assertion that John possesses a more or less well-defined disjunction of conjunctions of lion-like features. This would be the substitution theory in Boolean normal form.

---

under this same title any theory which holds that when a sentence is used metaphorically, at least some expression it contains undergoes a shift in meaning. Later I shall show that Max Black, Monroe Beardsley, and many others hold sophisticated versions of a meaning-shift theory.[2]

Opposed to meaning-shift theories, there are the *literalist* theories of, for example, Davidson and Searle. For both, 'John is a lion' just means that John is a lion, and is true just in case John is a lion. *Comparativists*, as I have described them, maintain that 'John is a lion,' when used metaphorically, is elliptical for 'John is like a lion.' Now it is important to see that this is also a *literalist* theory, since no shift in meaning takes place by treating one expression *A* as elliptical for another expression *B*. If *A* is elliptical for *B*, then it meant the same thing as *B* all along.

Given an analysis of metaphorical utterances, we would then expect a theory of metaphor to go on to explain how metaphors function, sometimes with extraordinary power, within a communicative situation. It will be a strong mark against an analysis of metaphors if, under that analysis, the force of metaphors becomes unintelligible.

Davidson and Searle produce what might be called *fecund falsehood* accounts of the force of metaphors. For both, metaphorical utterances mean just what they say, and, in the great majority of cases, what they say is false. Pressing this literalist theme is the main point of Davidson's essay, but, as we saw, he also indicates that recognizing the falsehood of the metaphorical utterance can lead us "to seek common features" (40), or "invite us to make comparisons" (40), that will often reveal likenesses that are

---

2. Nelson Goodman holds a nominalist variant of a meaning-shift theory, that is, such a theory cleansed of what Goodman considers improper references to meaning. As he says, "The treatment of metaphor in the following pages agrees in many matters with the excellent article by Max Black, 'Metaphor'" (*Languages*, 71n).

"novel and surprising" (33). Here, then, is a gesture in the direction of a causal theory of the way metaphors work. Why are metaphors often so powerful? I do not think Davidson addresses himself to this question.

Although Searle, like Davidson, is a literalist concerning what metaphors mean and adopts a fecund falsehood theory of how they work, his emphasis and positive theory are very different. Within the context of a speech act theory it is a commonplace that we can perform indirect speech acts using false statements as vehicles. (As I showed in chapter 2, irony and hyperbole function this way.) The central task for Searle is to spell out the principles that connect the direct speech act of uttering a false statement with the indirect speech act of producing a metaphor. Unlike Davidson, and this is a crucial difference, Searle does not invoke a causal theory. For him, the recognition of an intentional falsehood (where the speaker plainly does not intend to deceive) does not simply lead the respondent to make certain associations and comparisons; instead, the respondent becomes involved in the *cognitive* task of making sense out of the remark in a way that best preserves the integrity of the conversational exchange. I think that this is right, and importantly right, for making the respondent active in the comprehension of a metaphor helps to explain some of its rhetorical force.[3]

Turning now to Black: after he spends a great deal of time attacking what he calls the substitution and comparison views of metaphor, he offers in their place a version of a meaning-shift account of metaphor. The core of this position is given in the four following propositions:

> A metaphorical statement has two distinct subjects—a "principal" subject and a "subsidiary" one.

3. The rhetorical power gained by making the respondent a participant in determining the content of the indirect speech act was a central theme of chapter 2.

These subjects are best regarded as a "system" of things rather than "things."

The metaphor works by applying to the principal subject a system of "associated implications" characteristic of the subsidiary subject.

This involves shifts in meaning of words belonging to the same family or system as the metaphorical expression . . . ("Metaphor," 44–45)

Roughly, when a vocabulary from one context is applied to another context, then the interaction between these two contexts induces a change in meaning of the original vocabulary. Metaphorical meaning, then, is primary meaning displaced by the force field of the new context in which the utterance is used. At times, metaphors simply reproduce old meanings in a new and striking way. But metaphors can also produce genuinely new meanings, which, sometimes at least, will not admit of an adequate paraphrase into literal language.

Monroe Beardsley presents another version of the meaning-shift view of metaphors:

When a predicate is metaphorically adjoined to a subject, the predicate loses its ordinary extension, because it acquires a new intention—perhaps one it has in no other context. And this twist of meaning is forced by inherent tensions, or oppositions, within the metaphor itself. (294)

The first sentence in this passage clearly exhibits a commitment to a meaning-shift account of metaphors. I'll come back to this in a moment. The second sentence contains a more important claim: unlike the fecund falsehood theories of Searle and Davidson, the clash that triggers a figurative reading, or, for Beardsley, generates figurative meaning, is not between the statement and the context in which it is used; instead, the clash lies within the metaphorical utterance itself. Thus, for Beardsley, *oxymoron* becomes the model for metaphors:

> It should be counted as a merit in a theory of metaphor that it can analyze metaphor in the same terms that will do for oxymoron. (297–98)

Then more strongly:

> The truth seems . . . to be that in oxymoron we have the archetype, the most apparent and intense form, of verbal opposition. (298)

To see how this works, consider the oxymoron, 'silent scream': how do we recognize that it cannot be read literally? The answer is that being silent and being a scream are incompatible, virtually opposite, notions. How do we make sense of this puzzle? Beardsley suggests that we readjust the meaning of words: connotations that were candidates waiting to become criteria of meaning are elevated to that status, and old criteria are set (or pushed) aside. So in the expression 'silent scream,' one or both of the words it contains takes on a new meaning—at least for a while.

There is, then, an important difference in emphasis between Black's version of the meaning-shift theory and Beardsley's. For Black, a metaphor is a mechanism for imposing a categorical scheme from one domain onto another, a view that he presents even more strongly in his more recent writing on metaphor:

> I am now impressed, as I was insufficiently so when composing *Metaphor*, by the tight connection between the notions of models and metaphors. Each implication-complex supported by a metaphor's secondary subject, I now think, is a *model* of the ascriptions imputed to the primary subject. Every metaphor is the tip of a submerged model. ("More About Metaphor," 31)

Beardsley takes tension or opposition to be essential to metaphors. For both Beardsley and Black, however, metaphors are meaning generators.

Goodman, for his part, combines the interaction and opposition theories. Sounding rather like Beardsley, he tells us:

> a metaphor is an affair between a predicate with a past and an object that yields while protesting. . . . Application of a term is metaphorical only if to some extent it is contra-indicated. (*Languages*, 69)

Yet the dominant theme of Goodman's position is close to Black's interaction theory. With a metaphor, he tells us,

> A whole set of alternative labels, a whole apparatus of organization, takes over new territory. What occurs is a transfer of a schema, a migration of concepts, an alienation of categories. Indeed, a metaphor might be regarded as a calculated category mistake—or rather as a happy and revitalizing, even if bigamous, second marriage. (73)

The imagery of rape and the metaphor of infidelity bring out the two sides of Goodman's position.

Having given a sense of these sophisticated versions of a meaning-shift theory. I would like to side with Davidson in rejecting them.[4] With him, I do not find any of them convincing, because I do not think that words can be made to change meaning in the ways that Black, Beardsley, and others suggest. When I say ironically that it is cold in here, *I* might mean that it is hot in here, but the word 'cold' does not thereby come to mean hot. The same is true when words are used metaphorically.

There is, however, a profound problem with Davidson's view

---

4. Although Davidson (misguidedly, as I have argued) spends some time attacking the traditional comparativist account of metaphors, the chief point of his essay "What Metaphors Mean" is to reject the meaning-shift views of Black, Henle, Beardsley, and others.

that goes quite beyond the fact that he has yet to spell out the details of his own causal theory of metaphors. As Goodman has insisted against Davidson, it is a plain fact that we sometimes call sentences false when taken literally and true when taken metaphorically.[5] *What,* on Davidson's account, are we calling true when we say that a metaphorical utterance is true? Not the sentence literally taken, for that, after all, is (usually) false. But, on Davidson's theory, no other candidate presents itself; indeed, it is the essence of his theory to insist on this point:

> We must give up the idea that a metaphor carries a message, that it has a content or meaning (except, of course, its literal meaning). (45)

We seem now to be confronted with a dilemma. Meaning-shift theorists *can* give an account of the propriety of calling metaphorical utterances true.[6] What's true, they claim, is the utterance with its meaning metaphorically transformed. But Davidson insists, and I think that he is right in this, that this appeal to a shift in meaning makes no sense. On the other side, if we give up the meaning-shift theory, we seem to be at a loss, as I think Davidson is, to explain our normal practice of calling certain metaphorical utterances true.

What we want may, at first sight, seem impossible to get: a theory that allows us to say that an utterance when taken literally is false, but when taken metaphorically is true, even though there has been no shift in the meaning in these two ways of taking the utterance. In fact, however, the traditional elliptical-simile theory solves this dilemma in a straightforward and natural way. A metaphorical utterance of the form 'A is a ϕ' just means, and literally means, that A is like a ϕ. Likeness claims, however,

---

5. See his "Metaphors as Moonlighting," in Johnson, 222ff.

6. We also call metaphorical utterances *false,* and not simply on the basis of their literal falsehood.

have criteria of adequacy that shift with context. If someone says that A is like B in one context, and then says it again in another, then although he has said the same thing twice over (that A is like B), one of these utterances could be true while the other is false. If we like, we can still talk about a shift taking place, but it is not a shift in the meaning of words; it is a shift, as I shall argue in the next chapter, in the modes of relevance and evaluation governing the likeness claim.

A few words of summary. Despite the infighting, much of the recent discussion of metaphors has rested on two pillars: the rejection of the comparativist account of metaphors and the acceptance of some form of a meaning-shift theory. In the previous chapter I argued that the attacks on the comparativist position are, one and all, no good. In this chapter I have sided with Davidson in rejecting meaning-shift theories. This, I think, clears the deck.

6

A Theory of Figurative Comparisons

After a great deal of work we have arrived at the conclusion that there is no reason to abandon the traditional view that metaphors are elliptical similes. The claim seems prima facie plausible; there seem to be no valid criticisms against it; and no better theory exists to displace it. Since similes present *figurative* comparisons, treating metaphors as elliptical similes amounts to treating metaphors as figurative comparisons as well. This doesn't say much, of course, and it is a thesis worth defending in detail partly because it has been so often denied by recent writers. The claim is, however, systematically important in the following way: figurative language involves a departure from literal language, and this suggests that a study of figurative comparisons should begin with an examination of non-figurative comparisons. In line with this, in this chapter I shall try to answer three questions:

How do non-figurative comparisons function?
What are the mechanisms that give rise to figurative comparisons?
What explains the power of figurative comparisons?

NON-FIGURATIVE COMPARISONS

What are we saying when we claim that one thing is similar to (or like) another? It should be clear that we are not saying any of the following things: the two objects share at least one property; the two objects share a significantly large number of properties; the objects share at least one significant property; the objects share a sufficiently large number of significant properties. The argument from the asymmetry of many similarity statements shows that all of these views, with their reference to the symmetrical relation of *sharing*, must be incorrect. Following Tversky, a better suggestion might look like this: To say that A is similar to B means that A has a sufficiently large number of B's salient features. I do not, however, want to press this as an *analysis* of similarity statements since I am suspicious of making an explicit reference to salience within the analysis of similarity statements. Similarity claims do not seem to be assertions *about* salient features. It might be better to say that 'A is similar to B' just says that A has a sufficiently large number of qualities in common with B, with the additional side-constraint that the salient features of B establish the domain of features that are allowed to count. But I don't want to go into any of this in detail, since it is not necessary for my present purposes. I shall simply use the formula, 'A is similar to B just in case A has a sufficiently large number of B's salient features,'[1] in order to elucidate some aspects of similarity statements that are uncontroversial in themselves.

One feature of claims that A is similar to B (or even that A is similar to B in a given respect) is that they are factually lean or content-hungry. If I do not know Sally and Sue, and I am told Sally is like Sue (or even that Sally looks like Sue), I have been told something, but very little. Why, if they express so little content, do we make similarity claims at all? There are a number

1. Notice that on this approach, similarity is not a symmetrical relation since the salient features of B that A shares may not be salient features of A.

of answers to this. First, if I *do* know Sue, and understand the point of the comparison, then being told that Sally is like Sue may give me a great deal of detailed and valuable information in compact form. Suppose that Sue is an able scholar who has just been lost to another university, and Sally is a candidate to replace her. In that setting, being told, by someone who knows both, that Sally is like Sue could be very helpful indeed.

Using terminology borrowed from Searle, we can say that similarity claims typically gain their force as indirect speech acts. When we say that *A* is like *B*, we are indicating that *A* has a sufficiently large number of *B*'s salient features, relative, of course, to the interests of the present context, and the point of saying this is usually to convey specific information about *A*.[2] If Sue is an able scholar, fine teacher, and amiable colleague, then being told that Sally is like Sue conversationally implies (or indirectly asserts) that she has a good share of these salient features as well. I think that the chief use (or, at least, a chief use) of similarity statements is to convey factual information in just this indirect manner.

I think that a second reason why likeness statements are useful is that they solve (or help to solve) what might be called the ineffability problem. For example, it is often difficult to describe a face in a way that captures its particular look. Try it with Bette Davis. Yet if I say that someone looks like Bette Davis, I may succeed in giving someone quite a good idea of what that person looks like; and I do this even though I could not produce a particularly good word picture of either Bette Davis or the person who is said to look like her. I suspect that one reason comparisons (metaphors, similes) so often appear in literature is precisely that they provide ways of solving problems of ineffability.[3]

2. I say this is *usually* the point of making comparisons because I want to acknowledge the existence of other uses of similarity claims; for example, to record a likeness (say between two faces) that we find striking.
3. In his essay "Why Metaphors Are Necessary and Not Just Nice,"

Now if one of the main tasks of similarity claims is to convey information, we would expect them to be controlled by standard Gricean maxims governing the cooperative exchange of information. It is easy to show that this is true. To illustrate this, I will let uppercase letters indicate salient features, lowercase letters non-salient features. One way that a comparison of Sally with Sue can go wrong is by suggesting that Sally has one of Sue's salient features when she does not:

Ia	Sally	Sue
	$\sim f$	F

Perhaps Sue is a gifted linguist, and Sally is not. The situation would be worse if Sally's lack of feature f was one of her salient features:

Ib	Sally	Sue
	$\sim F$	F

In these cases, we can say that the comparison indirectly *mis*-describes Sally by attributing to her a feature she lacks. This is very close to a violation of Grice's rule of quality, "Do not say what you believe to be false" ("Logic," 46), for if the person had asserted directly that Sally is f, then that assertion would have been false.

A second way in which the comparison can be inappropriate is for Sue to lack one of Sally's salient features.

IIa	Sally	Sue
	F	$\sim f$

Andrew Ortony speaks of a *Compactness Thesis*, which corresponds to the first point made above, and an *Inexpressibility Thesis*, which corresponds to my second point. Our only difference is that I do not restrict these theses to metaphors, but apply them to all comparisons, both figurative and non-figurative.

At first glance, it may seem that this second way in which a comparison can be inappropriate is identical with the first way. But this is wrong. Since Sally is being compared with Sue, the salient features of Sue's feature space dominate. In case IIa, we can say that Sue has been indirectly *under*-described, and this parallels a violation of Grice's rule of quantity, "Make your contribution as informative as is required (for the current purposes of the exchange)" ("Logic," 45). Of course, if Sue *saliently* lacks f, then we get this pattern:

IIb	Sally	Sue
	F	~F

and once more we have a counterpart of a violation of the Gricean rule of quality.

Turning to more subtle ways in which comparisons can go wrong, consider these cases:

III	Sally	Sue
	f	F
IV	Sally	Sue
	F	f

Here we might say that there is a mismatch of salience. In III, one of Sally's non-salient features is inappropriately played up, and in IV, one of her salient features is inappropriately played down. In both cases we might grudgingly admit that what is being said is true, but still out of focus and possibly quite misleading. By placing prominence in the wrong place or by not placing it in the right place, we get something like a violation of Grice's rule of relevance, "Be relevant" ("Logic," 46), but I will not insist upon this.[4]

To summarize, when a comparison is used to convey information, the speaker is expected to find an object of comparison which provides a good match with the subject that is being compared to it. The respondent is typically thought to be lacking in relevant information concerning the subject of comparison, but is thought to be appropriately informed concerning the salient features of the object to which the subject is being compared. Given the first feature without the second, the comparison will be true, but ineffective for the exchange of information. Given the second feature without the first, the comparison will effectively propagate false or misleading information.

Before turning to figurative comparisons, I wish to look briefly at a second use of comparative judgments: their employment to *call attention to* likenesses and similarities.[5] This is an important activity in courts of law where arguments often depend on the question of which precedents are similar (or most similar) to the extant case. Connoisseurship also depends upon detecting likenesses: the echoes of Ingres in Picasso, the Schubertean themes in Scott Joplin, and so forth.

We could, of course, still say that comparisons of this kind provide information about the subject, namely, that the subject resembles the object, but the stress is altogether different from that in the information-giving use of comparisons. In the information-giving use of comparisons, the central fract is that the respondent has relevant information about the object of comparison and lacks it with respect to the subject of comparison, and the comparison is invoked in order to overcome this lack. When a

4. It is also evident that comparisons are governed by Grice's rule of manner, "Be perspicuous," with its submaxims, "Avoid obscurity of expression; avoid ambiguity; etc." ("Conversation," 46).

5. We shall see later that this use of similarity claims is rather more relevant to figurative comparisons than is the information-giving use.

comparison is used to call attention to a likeness, the speaker assumes that the respondent has relevant information about both the object and the subject of comparison.

These remarks demand elaboration and qualification. First of all, even when the point of a comparison is to call attention to a likeness, the direction of match must still go from object to subject, and hence the likeness claim will often be asymmetrical. Again, beach chairs look like clothespins, but not the other way around. Secondly, as far as I can tell, comparisons used to draw attention to similarities are still governed by Grice-like maxims concerning good fit. This, as we shall see, marks an important difference between the use of figurative and non-figurative comparisons.

One qualification: the information-giving and the attention-calling uses of similarity claims are not always easily separated. When an art historian calls attention to Giottesque features in a fresco by Masaccio, the student may for the first time notice the sculptural qualities of Masaccio's figures which are, indeed, similar to Giotto's. Yet the basic contrast remains unaltered: there is an important difference between comparing S with O in order assert a similarity between them, and asserting a similarity between S and O in order to convey information about S using O as a vehicle.

EXPLICIT AND IMPLICIT COMPARISONS

Many of our comparisons, both figurative and non-figurative, are expressed elliptically by dropping the phrase 'is like.' But as I showed in chapter 3, there are other ways of drawing comparisons indirectly. We can, for example, draw or evoke comparisons between A and B by referring to A as a B or by speaking about A as if it were a B. Lakoff and Johnson supply an example of this second mode of implicit comparison when they point out that we

speak about *arguments* using the language of *war* and *battles*.[6]
We *attack* the *weak points* in our *opponent's position*. We *win* and
lose arguments. We try to *hoist an opponent on his own petard*.
And so on. In the same way, Shakespeare does not say that time is
(like) a person and then go on to indicate in which ways; he simply
says:

> Time hath, my lord, a wallet at his back
> Wherein he puts alms for oblivion,
> *Troilus and Cressida* (Act III, sc. 3, 1.145)

We can, in fact, treat these implicit comparisons as deep
ellipses:

A is (like B in respect) r.   Time is like a person
                                     with a wallet at his
                                     back.

becomes:

A is r.   Time hath a wallet at his
                                     back.

I do not think that this elliptical analysis sheds any light on the
power of this metaphor, but it is not intended to. Such an
expansion can also deaden the line. The only point that I am
trying to make is that the respondent treats these passages as
implicit comparisons and would be stupefied by them if he did
not.

Actually, these last remarks, though perhaps true, are misleading in suggesting that we *begin* with independent notions of
time and persons and then compare them. In fact, as Lakoff and
Johnson have argued persuasively, our concept of time is shaped

6. George Lakoff and Mark Johnson, "Conceptual Metaphor in Everyday Life," *The Journal of Philosophy* 77 (1980): 453–486. Reprinted
in Johnson, *Philosophical Perspectives on Metaphor*. Page references are to
this second source (288ff).

by the system of comparisons *conventionally* associated with it. For us, time is something characterized by spatial features, personal features, features of motion, et cetera. This system of conventional and standard comparisons determines, in part, at least, the *literal* meaning of our temporal language (288ff.).

Lakoff and Johnson argue, again I think persuasively, that these conventional systems of comparisons are a pervasive feature of our language and they both reflect and constitute elemental features of our *Lebenswelt* (Heidegger's word, not theirs). To cite one of their more striking examples, we live most of our lives upright, and, with some notable exceptions, lie down only when we are inactive, sick, injured, or dead. This leads, they argue, to endless manifestations of the principle, "UP IS GOOD, DOWN IS BAD" (298).

I think that all of this is fascinating, for it shows, among other things, both the pervasiveness and the power of systems of comparisons. I would, however, like to raise an objection to their way of speaking that is more than terminological. Where I have spoken of *comparisons,* Lakoff and Johnson usually speak of *metaphors,* characterizing them this way:

> The essence of metaphor is understanding and experiencing one kind of thing or experience in terms of another. (289)

On this account, any comparison, however flat-footedly literal, will count as a metaphor, and that, it seems to me, is not how we use the word 'metaphor.'

But what difference does it make if we expand the notion of a metaphor to encompass all comparisons? First of all, it gives a specious air of originality and paradox to the underlying thesis that Lakoff and Johnson are attempting to further. They picture other linguists and philosophers of language who have given preference to the *literal* over the *merely metaphorical,* now being forced to admit that the literal is based on the metaphorical, not

the other way around. This is misleading (and speciously excit-
ing), because metaphorical language is traditionally taken to be a
type of *figurative* language, and it is startling to be told that the
literal is based on the figurative. To put it soberly, however,
Lakoff and Johnson have not shown, as they claim, *that most of
our normal conceptual system is metaphorically structured* (312)
but instead, *that most of our normal conceptual systems is structured through comparisons*. With this rephrasing, a seeming
paradox is replaced by a claim that probably no one will deny,
even if it hasn't been taken seriously enough.

Expanding the notion of metaphor to include all comparisons
has a second, more unfortunate, consequence: metaphors, as
traditionally understood, become peripheral and largely ignored.
We thus find Lakoff and Johnson contrasting "literal metaphors"
(308) with metaphors that are part of "figurative" or "imaginative"
language (307). And we find sentences like this:

> On the other hand, metaphorical concepts can be extend-
> ed beyond the range of ordinary literal ways of thinking
> and talking into the range of what is called figurative,
> poetic, colorful, or fanciful thought and language. (294)

With the arresting thought that metaphors can *also* be used
figuratively, Lakoff and Johnson return to explaining what they
take to be the primary, that is, the literal, uses of metaphors.
What this shows, I believe, is that Lakoff and Johnson share the
intellectualist prejudices against metaphors—*real* metaphors—that they are so fond of attributing to others.

I think that it is worthwhile to insist on these points because it
is important to unmask enemies disguised as friends. More
deeply, I think that Lakoff and Johnson have said interesting
things about literal (non-figurative, non-metaphorical) comparisons, and since figurative comparisons use non-figurative comparisons as their base, an understanding of one will help in the
understanding of the other.

FIGURATIVE COMPARISONS

In the first part of this study, we saw that a central feature of a whole series of tropes (including irony, hyperbole, and meiosis) is a mutually recognized intention by the speaker that the respondent not take the speaker's words at face value, but, instead, replace them with a correct judgment. In all these figures of speech, the speaker is trying to induce in the respondent a (mutually recognized) adjustment or replacement of what the speaker actually said. I wish to suggest that something very similar takes place with figurative comparisons.

According to one popular view of metaphors (championed by Searle and Davidson, among others), the claim that Margaret Thatcher is a bulldozer is false just because, after all, she is not a bulldozer. I have rejected this quick and easy argument, for it seems to me that the claim that Margaret Thatcher is a bulldozer should be treated as an alternative way of saying that Margaret Thatcher is *like* a bulldozer. How about that statement; is *it* true or false? If we allow the standard salient features of bulldozers to fix the relevant feature space, then the judgment is surely *false*. Margaret Thatcher cannot, for example, move huge quantities of dirt in an efficient manner. Of course, if someone describes her as a bulldozer, he will not expect his respondents to interpret his remark straightforwardly in a bulldozer-salient feature space. The reason he does not expect this is that in such a feature space, his remark is a pointless and mutually recognized falsehood. He speaks, to return to the central theme of chapter 2, in order to call forth a (mutually recognized) adjustment or correction.

There are, however, important differences between the ways in which figurative predications call forth corrections and figurative comparisons do this. With figurative predications, the context is held steady, and the assertion made within that context is adjusted or corrected. With figurative comparisons, the comparison is not rejected; the claim that *A* is like *B* is not withdrawn,

corrected, or modified in any way. Instead, the context is adjusted to accommodate it. This idea comes from Tversky, who puts it
this way:

> There is a close tie between the assessment of similarity
> and the interpretation of metaphors. In judgments of
> similarity one assumes a particular feature space, or a
> frame of reference, and assesses the quality of the match
> between the subject and the referent. In the interpreta-
> tion of similes, one assumes a resemblance between the
> subject and the referent and searches for an interpreta-
> tion of the space that would maximize the quality of the
> match. The same pair of objects, therefore, can be
> viewed as similar or different depending on the choice of
> a frame of reference. (349)

I think that this passage may overly intellectualize the procedure
of metaphor and simile interpretation, but it seems to me that its
central point provides the key for a correct account of the function
of figurative comparisons.

To see this consider the three following claims:

A road grader is like a bulldozer.
Margaret Thatcher is like a bulldozer.
Shirley Temple was like a bulldozer.

The first statement is literally true. Like bulldozers, road graders
are also used to push about large quantities of dirt, the chief
difference being that road graders have their blades beneath their
chassis rather than in front of them. The second sentence, I have
said, is literally false, yet there are people who would consider it
true if taken figuratively. How might they arrive at this opinion?
Tversky has a suggestion that bears directly on this point:

> It appears that people interpret similes by scanning the
> feature space and selecting the features of the referent
> that are applicable to the subject (e.g., by selecting

features of the bulldozer that are applicable to the person). (349)

Here we seem to be involved in a two-step process. By comparing a person with a bulldozer, we invoke a feature space dominated by bulldozer-salient qualities. But under that reading, the comparison seems plainly false. In order to avoid attributing a pointlessly false statement to the speaker, the respondent now prunes the feature space of the falsifying features and, if the metaphor is *sound* (I'm not saying *striking*; I'll come back to that later), then the comparison, figuratively taken, is true.

I think that this account is still too simple, and qualifications and elaborations are needed, but it does seem to yield the correct result that the third statement, the one about Shirley Temple, is false taken both literally and figuratively. Taken literally, Shirley Temple's features provide a bad match with the unpruned set of bulldozer-salient features, and the bad match persists even after the feature space is pruned back to salient features relevant to humans.

Even in this simple form, this approach goes some way in answering basic questions about metaphors and similes. First, what does the figurativeness of a figurative comparison amount to? Figurativeness is a departure from the literal. In the first part of this study, we saw that one way a speaker can depart from literalness is to say something with the mutually understood intention that the utterance not be taken at face value, but instead, be adjusted or corrected so that *it squares with the context*. With metaphors and similes, the respondent is given the mutually recognized task of *squaring the context with the utterance*. Though these mechanisms work in reverse fashion, they have this in common: the target thought-act or speech-act is produced in the respondent as part of his participatory response, rather than merely given to him in the form of the speaker's direct speech act. This, I think, is part of the reason that metaphors and similes often have more force than counterpart descriptions (when such are available).

Returning now to the two uses of non-figurative comparisons—the *information-giving* and the *likeness-noting*—it seems evident that metaphors and similes most resemble, or are typically instances of, the likeness-noting use. With the likeness-noting use of a comparison, the respondent is presumed to be acquainted with both objects of comparison, and in metaphors, again, two antecedently known things are brought into comparison. There is, however, an important difference between literal likeness-noting comparisons (for example, 'Churchill looked like a bulldog') and figurative likeness-noting comparisons (for example, 'Churchill was [like] a bulldog'). In the first case, the characteristic physiognomy of a bulldog face establishes the criterion of comparison, and, if the comparison is correct, then Churchill's face must meet it. Here it might be objected that in making this comparison, we set aside all sorts of bulldog-face features: fur, wet nose, and so forth. These, however, are not *salient* features of a bulldog's face since they do not set it off from the faces of other dogs. That, I think, is why it can be right to say that Churchill looked like a bulldog, but wrong to say that he looked like a dog. [7]

The situation is different in metaphorically saying that Churchill is (like) a bulldog, though the fact that this is a dead metaphor will somewhat mute this point. Encountering such a comparison for the first time, we would certainly be struck by its impropriety, for bulldogs possess a great many salient features that Churchill lacks: for example, having a very strong (not just square) jaw, being small enough to crawl into burrows, et cetera. It is this transparent incongruity that leads us, in Beardsley's words, to

7. There could be contexts in which it would be appropriate to say that Churchill looks like a dog rather than, say, a cat. (Ted Cohen pointed this out to me.) In general, however, it is wrong to reason as follows: ϕ is a salient feature of As; all As are Bs; therefore ϕ is a salient feature of Bs. For this reason, x can look like an A, where all As are Bs, yet not look like a B.

give our reading a 'metaphorical twist.' But over against Beardsley and the other meaning-shift theorists (Black, Henle, and
others) the twist does not alter the meaning of any expression;
instead, as Tversky suggests, the order of dominance in salient
features is reversed.[8] In calling Churchill a bulldog, we compare
him to a bulldog (as opposed, say, to a French poodle), while at
the same time trimming the feature space in terms of the subject's
salient features.

At this point I return to the dilemma raised at the close of the
previous chapter. There I asked how it could be possible for an
utterance to be false when taken literally, but true when taken
metaphorically without there being any shift of meaning from the
one reading to the other. I can first note that parallel situations
arise with non-figurative language. If I say "I am James Jones,"
and James Jones says "I am James Jones," then, unless I happen
to be named James Jones, what I say is false and what he says is
true, even though there is no shift in the meanings of the words
used.[9] Less controversially, and closer to the present case, if 'x is
good' means something like 'x satisfies relevant standards of
evaluation,' then saying that x is good could be true in some
contexts, but not in others, without there being any shift in the
meaning of what is said. This, it seems to me, is how likeness
claims—both literal and figurative—function: what they say is
that one thing is like another, and whether that's true or not will
depend upon canons of similarity determined by the context.
Along with its naturalness, I think that one of the chief strengths

8. The repeated use of a metaphorical expression can, however, shift
(alter, expand, and so on) the meaning of a term. This happens when a
metaphor becomes frozen or dies. Through repeated use, the metaphor's
indirect figurative meaning becomes a new literal meaning and the metaphor dies, as a number of writers have said, of its own success.

9. There is, of course, a shift in the reference of the word 'I'; thus
people who (wrongly, I think) make the meaning of an indexical a function
of its reference will find this example unpersuasive.

of the elliptical-simile theory is that it can explain how a sentence taken literally can be false, while the sentence taken metaphorically can be true, without invoking the implausible idea that, when used metaphorically, words change their meaning.

I have argued that metaphors, like similes, are figurative comparisons, and in this chapter I have tried to explain how figurative comparisons work. They function the way other likeness-noting comparisons function, with a radical difference in the character of the matching relationship between the subject and object of comparison. Before closing, I wish to raise two further questions: (i) why do figurative comparisons often carry considerable rhetorical force? and (ii) why are they such a powerful intellectual and aesthetic resource?

The answer to the first question parallels the answer to the same question concerning irony, hyperbole, and meiosis. Figurative comparisons gain rhetorical force through inducing in the respondent a mutually recognized correction. The point of a figurative comparison is to draw attention to or perhaps create a certain likeness or system of likenesses. Through figurativeness, the respondent is made to arrive at the result himself. I think that this is what Aristotle had in mind when he compared metaphors to puzzles; and a puzzle, of course, loses a great deal when presented together with its solution.

The second question—why figurative comparisons provide such a powerful intellectual and aesthetic resource—has a number of answers. To begin with, *non*-figurative comparisons possess these features, and figurative comparisons build upon them. Comparisons, we have seen, help us to overcome problems of ineffability by allowing us to make connections when there is no direct way of saying what the connection is. Metaphors extend this capacity by allowing us to make connections even when no straightforward comparison is available.[10] Second, like irony,

10. This point may help to answer a problem put to me by Stanley Eveling: how, on the present account, are we to explain the *private* use of

metaphor is a simple device that admits of endless sophisticated elaboration. I think this is worth saying in order to take some of the mystery out of metaphor. The power of metaphor lies in those who can use this device in a creative and insightful way. The next chapter contains reflections on how this takes place.

---

metaphors, that is, those occasions where a person uses a metaphor simply for his own personal amusement or edification? The answer, I think, is that comparisons in general, and figurative comparisons in particular, provide a way of making manifest relations that could not—or could not easily—be made manifest in other ways.

7

Clarifications and Elaborations

At various places I have fallen in with others by speaking about the metaphorical or figurative meaning of some expression. There is really nothing wrong with speaking in this way except that it might suggest that an expression can have two distinct meanings, a literal meaning and a metaphorical (or figurative) meaning, and that, in turn, might suggest a commitment to a meaning-shift theory of metaphors of the kind I reject.

SOME CLARIFICATIONS

The easiest way to clarify these matters is to look first at non-figurative comparisons. Typically, the point of the *direct* speech act of saying that *A* is like *B* is given in the *indirect* speech act that indicates that *A* has a certain feature salient in *B*. I say that Smith is like Jones in order to indicate that Smith (like Jones) is affable if not particularly bright. If asked what I meant by saying that Smith is like Jones, I might actually reply that I meant that Smith is affable, if not particularly bright. That's what *I* meant, though of course that's not what my *words* meant.

With figurative comparisons, as with literal comparisons, the point of the comparison lies in the indirect speech act—what I mean rather than simply what my words mean. But the difference between a figurative and a non-figurative comparison does not consist in some new kind of meaning being conveyed, figurative meaning rather than literal meaning. Here we would do better to drop the expression 'figurative meaning' altogether and speak instead of someone *putting forward* a claim figuratively rather than literally. With non-figurative comparisons, the speaker seeks a good fit that will facilitate the easy transfer of accurate information. More fully, the speaker offers his comparisons under the restraints of Gricean conversational maxims. With a figurative comparison the speaker flouts, or at least violates, standard conversational rules and thus engages the respondent in the task of making adjustments that will produce a good fit. The difference here is not between two kinds of meaning, but rather between two modes of entertaining and validating a comparison. Speakers speak figuratively, but words do not have figurative meanings.[1]

These remarks provide an opportunity to say something more about the problem of paraphrase. The comparativist has no difficulty in giving a paraphrase of the metaphorical expression 'A is a ϕ.' It just means, literally means, that A is like a ϕ. Critics seem to think, however, that somehow the comparativist is committed to giving an adequate paraphrase of the content of the

---

1. For a detailed elaboration of ideas along these lines, see Ted Cohen's fine essay "Figurative Speech and Figurative Acts." Though I have no reason to suppose that Cohen would accept my defense of the classical comparativist position, his own development of a speech-act account of metaphors with its emphasis on the *perlocutionary* force of figurative utterances strikes me as the right way to proceed in this area. Again, however, as indicated in the first chapter, I have chosen not to develop the present account of figurative language at this degree of theoretical specificity since this is liable to raise difficult and controversial issues that need not be reached for the purposes of this work.

indirect speech act that may be the point of the comparison. This simply is not true, and, again, the point can be made with respect to *non*-figurative comparisons. I say that someone runs like a gazelle to indicate that he runs with effortless speed and grace. If asked if that is what I meant, I may say yes, feeling that nothing, or at least nothing important, has been left out. At other times, because of the problems of ineffability discussed in the previous chapter, no literal paraphrase can be found that captures the content of the intended indirect speech act in an adequate way. Perhaps figurativeness increases ineffability, but it is important to see that ineffability can exist even before comparisons are subjected to a metaphorical twist.

But to return to the central point, comparativists are often challenged to produce literal paraphrases of what, after all, is the content of the intended indirect speech act. This can be done with varying degrees of success, and it is sometimes *very* useful to try to do this, but the success or failure of these efforts has no bearing on the correctness of the comparativist accounts of metaphors.

Turning to another point, throughout I have defended what has been called the elliptical-simile account of metaphors. I think that this is a perfectly good way of describing (or naming) the position I hold except for the fact that its critics have the persistent bad habit of forgetting that similes present *figurative* comparisons. Another way of stating my position that would avoid this possible misunderstanding is to say that *both* metaphors and similes present figurative comparisons. This way of speaking has, in fact, been tacitly adopted in much of this work.

Aside from avoiding misunderstandings, there might be some other advantages in speaking of a theory of figurative comparisons rather than, more narrowly, about an elliptical-simile theory of metaphors. This approach would play down the merely accidental ways in which a comparison can be put forward. Whether we say Achilles is like a lion, say he is a lion, refer to him as a lion, or speak about him as if he were a lion, we are drawing a comparison (a figurative comparison) between him and a lion. How the comparison is couched grammatically is of relatively less importance.

Finally, introducing the generic notion of a figurative comparison can bring out similarities between figures of speech, or other literary devices, that are often thought remote from each other. Satires and parodies also exploit figurative comparisons, sometimes in very sophisticated ways. Now that does not mean that satires are metaphors, although speaking that way can have a specious ring of profundity. It is easy to understand the temptation to let one member of a family of concepts become the representative of all the rest. (Sometimes all figurative language is referred to as being *ironic*.) There are, however, interesting relationships between metaphors and satires that could be explored in a developed theory of figurative comparisons.

ELABORATIONS

Recent writers on metaphor often insist, sometimes in extravagant terms, on the power of metaphors. They also complain about the prejudice against metaphor that springs, they suggest, from a narrow, literalist (positivist) conception of language. The fact of the matter is that the vast majority of metaphors are routine and uninteresting. Many metaphors are lame, misleading, overblown, inaccurate, et cetera. Metaphors, in indicating that one thing is like another, so far say very little. Their strength, which they share with comparisons in general, is that their near-emptiness makes them adaptable for use in a wide variety of contexts. On the reverse side, the near-emptiness of metaphors also makes them serviceable for those occasions when we want to avoid saying, and perhaps thinking, what we really mean. Euphemisms are typically couched in metaphors. Metaphors can be evasions—including poetic evasions. There are occasions when the poet must reject them and

Trace the gold sun about the whitened sky
Without evasion by a single metaphor.
Look at it in its essential barrenness
And say this, this is the centre that I seek.
                    Wallace Stevens, *Credences of Summer*

It is important, then, to calm down about metaphors. Some
are good; some are bad. Some are illuminating; some are obfus-
cating. For the most part they are routine. Furthermore, with
differences of emphasis, they all work in the same way: they
present a comparison with a transparent incongruity (oddness)
that admits of resolution. In Goodman's words:

> Metaphorical force requires a combination of novelty
> with fitness, of the odd with the obvious. (*Languages* 79)

This suggests that metaphors (and figurative comparisons in
general) can vary along two axes:

Without the incongruity or oddness, we would not be dealing with
a *figurative* comparison; and, quite obviously, unless this oddity
is resolved by a compensating comparison, we would not be
dealing with a figurative *comparison*—though we might be deal-

ing with another form of figurative language, perhaps irony, which has its own form of incongruity resolution.

Though both dimensions are necessary for metaphors, the stress can vary, producing metaphors with different tonalities.[2] It will be useful to give a rough geography of the ways in which metaphors are distributed through this two-dimensional space.

Metaphors of Wit. Aristotle compared metaphors with puzzles (*Poetics*, 1405b, 4–6), and by this he meant that the speaker presents the respondent with something to be solved. I do not know whether the Greek text supports this reading, but in English, at least, there is an important difference between a puzzle and a problem. Problems can be difficult to solve, but puzzles, at least good puzzles, are supposed to be baffling. Furthermore, solving a puzzle often depends upon seeing things in the right way, and after this is done, the solution then seems obvious. The charm of such puzzles consists in this transition from bafflement to an ingenious, though after the fact obvious, solution.

What I am calling metaphors of wit work in much the same way: the strength of the metaphor does not lie in the richness of the comparison, but in the pleasure of seeing an initial conflict resolved. There are two ways that this might be done. In the first, the respondents are supposed to supply the resolution themselves; in the second, the speaker (poet) produces the resolution to the amazement of the respondent. As an example of the first kind of metaphor of wit, consider Hegel's description of Schelling's system as "a night in which all cows are black." What he meant, of course, is that Schelling's system is so obscure that it is as difficult to comprehend its features as it is to distinguish black

2. Corresponding to these different types of metaphors, there are two different kinds of theories of metaphor: those that stress the dimension of incongruity or oddness (for example, the verbal-opposition theory of Beardsley), and those that stress the richness of the comparison (for example, the interaction or model theory of metaphors championed by Black).

cows on a dark night. Furthermore, the force of this metaphor does not depend on an illumination gained by applying nocturnal and bovine schemata to a philosophical system. For a metaphor of this kind, and it is, after all, a good metaphor, it seems completely overblown to say, as Goodman does:

> A whole set of alternative labels, a whole apparatus of organization, takes over a new territory. What occurs is a transfer of schema, a migration of concepts, an alienation of categories, etc. (*Languages*, 73)

Some metaphors may function in this way, but not all of them—and certainly not Hegel's.

Recent writers on metaphor tend to play down this use of figurative language, I suppose because it seems to reinforce the idea that metaphorical language is merely decorative. Of course, to say that figurative language is sometimes used for decorative purposes does not mean that it is always and only used for these purposes. Beyond this, it would be interesting to know the source of this peculiar intellectual prejudice against the decorative. A great many good poetic metaphors have simple and unproblematic literal explications that bring out the point of the metaphor. Sometimes, at least, "True wit is nature to advantage dress'd, / What oft was thought, but ne'er so well express'd / (Pope, *Essay on Criticism*, Pt. II, l. 97).

In the second kind of metaphor of wit, the speaker (poet) produces a comparison that is so farfetched, remote, or incongruous, that it seems impossible that it could be made good. Then, against all odds, the speaker does so. This example comes from Monty Python.

> WHISTLER (to the Prince of Wales): Your Majesty is like a
>   stream of bat's piss.
> PRINCE OF WALES: What?!
> WHISTLER: It was Wilde's.

WILDE: It certainly was not; it was Shaw's.
PRINCE OF WALES: Well, Mr. Shaw?
SHAW: I merely meant, your Majesty, that you shine out
   like a shaft of gold when all around is dark.[3]

Metaphors of wit make their leap to immortality in the writings of the metaphysical poets where the *argument* of the poem vindicates a wholly improbable comparison. These lines are from John Donne's "A Valediction: Forbidding Mourning," where he tells his lover that, though they must part, their souls will remain together:

> If they be two, they are two so
>   As stiff twin compasses are two;
> Thy soul, the fixed foot, makes no show
>   To move, but doth, if th' other do.
>
> And though it in the center sit,
>   Yet when the other far doth roam,
> It leans, and hearkens after it,
>   And grows erect, as that comes home.
>
> Such wilt thou be to me, who must
>   Like th' other foot, obliquely run;
> Thy firmness make my circle just,
>   And make me end where I begun.

I shall not attempt to analyze this poem in detail, but I wish to make two points concerning it. First, it contains a remarkably ingenious figurative comparison, but its poetic force is not nearly exhausted by the ingenuity with which an improbable comparison is made good. Remote comparisons, however well cashed in, can still make bad poetry. Second, although it would not be easy, and perhaps not possible, to produce an accurate paraphrase of this

3. *The Monty Python Instant Record Collection*, Vol. 2, Side A, Final Cut.

poem, its value does not consist in revealing truths that could not otherwise be expressed. Its value does not consist in revealing hitherto unknown or unappreciated features of love by presenting them through the filter of another system of relationships. The poem elevates and refreshes a series of commonplaces concerning the unity of separated lovers by bringing them together under a single surprising, though remarkably apt, image.

Again, since passions run high in this area, I should repeat that I am not making a claim about all metaphors, only those I have labeled metaphors of wit, that is, those figurative comparisons that gain their chief force by introducing, then resolving, deeply incongruous or unexpected comparisons. Such metaphors occur in both comic and serious poetry. They present paradigm cases of metaphors, and any complete theory of metaphors must explain them. Not surprisingly, they are well explained by a verbal opposition or tension theory of the kind that Beardsley championed, and not explained (and usually ignored) in the interaction theories of Black and Goodman.

Metaphors as Models. By metaphors as models, I mean those metaphors that gain their chief strength by imposing a system of relations from one domain onto another. This, as we have seen, is made a definitive feature of metaphors by Black, and he is largely followed in this by Goodman. For them metaphors present models that reveal, and perhaps create, characteristics that have often gone unrecognized and, perhaps, could not have been presented in any other, more direct, mode of discourse.[4]

---

4. As Black realizes, his later essay "More About Metaphor" takes a stronger position than his earlier essay "Metaphor." In "Metaphor" he says:

> The effect, then, of (metaphorically) calling a man a "wolf" is to evoke the wolf-system of related commonplaces (41).

In "Metaphor" the emphasis is mainly on the *related commonplaces*. In the second essay, where metaphors are called 'models' and compared with

Concentrating on Black and Goodman, who are the most articulate representatives of this interaction or model theory of metaphors, it is worth noting that neither chances his hand by illustrating the power of the position with a detailed examination of a genuinely rich example of poetic discourse. Black *cites* some interesting examples, for instance,

Light is but the shadow of God (Sir Thomas Browne),

but prefers to concentrate on more mundane examples such as, 'The chairman ploughed through the discussion,' and the old favorite, 'Man is a wolf.'

Actually, the metaphors Black examines do not provide particularly apt examples for a model theory of metaphor. Speaking of the chairman *ploughing* through the discussion does not superimpose an agricultural schema on the principal subject, that is, the activities of the chairman. The metaphor does not rely, for example, on fine distinctions among ploughing, disking, furrowing, and so forth. All that one has to know to appreciate the force of this expired metaphor is that a plough is a relatively crude instrument that turns soil by moving straight ahead. Similarly, we might want to say that calling a man a wolf "is to invoke the wolf-system of related commonplaces," but it is, after all, quite a thin system of commonplaces. If the model theory of metaphors is correct, then these examples fit it, at most, as limiting cases.

The passage from Sir Thomas Browne, which Black cites but does not discuss, is interestingly more complex. Calling light a shadow is an oxymoron, and, like most oxymorons, unpacks into a proportional metaphor:

God is to light as light is to shadow.

Here we certainly find more structure, but of a kind that illustrates the much maligned comparativist (not interactionist) view

---

theories, the emphasis shifts to the notion of a *system*. Here I am interested in this second, stronger, position which Black shares with Goodman.

of metaphors. Of course, we could say that every comparison involves modeling one thing by another, but then, of course, it is hard to understand why defenders of interaction/model theories have spent so much time attacking the traditional position.

We find cases where the model theory finds plausible application if we move away from metaphors (narrowly conceived) and examine such extended comparisons as analogies, parables, and allegories. Shakespeare provides a number of examples of extended figurative comparisons of this kind. "All the world's a stage," he tells us, and then proceeds to use the vocabulary of the stage to elucidate the nature of the human condition. In *Coriolanus*, Agrippa produces a parable of the parts of the body rebelling against the stomach as an argument against political insurrection, thus invoking the root metaphor of the organic conception of the state. In these cases, one area is understood through a system of terms drawn from another, and the model theory finds a non-trivial application.

It is worth noting that in each of these examples from Shakespeare, the level of *incongruity* is not very high. There are, of course, many ways in which the world is not like a stage (the world is not closed on Mondays), and similarly many ways in which an individual's relationship to the state is not like the relationship of a part of the body to the total organism. Yet these comparisons are not shocking, since compensating similarities are easily found. In general, as the weight of the figurative comparison shifts to the richness and strength of the comparison itself, the level of figurativeness generated by incongruity will diminish. This is not surprising, because a rich comparison seeks a good fit, whereas incongruity cuts against it. [5] When incongruity

5. The occasional genius can combine both dimensions to a high degree. The best example I know is Plato's presentation of the combined analogies of the divided line and the cave in the *Republic*. For an explication and celebration of these two analogies, see the author's "Three Platonic Analogies."

disappears altogether, figurativeness disappears with it.[6] Figurative comparisons, then, shade off into two different regions:

1. As incongruity dominates and the demand for a compensating rich comparison diminishes, figurative comparisons shade off into other figures of speech, for example, irony.
2. As the demand for a rich system of accurate comparisons dominates, and the incongruity (inner tension) diminishes, figurative comparisons shade off into complex literal comparisons, theories, or conceptual schemes.

Because of the first fact some philosophers (for example, Goodman) are tempted to think of irony as a mode of metaphor. The second fact has led others (for example, Black[7]) to suppose that a scientific theory is a kind of metaphor.

It may seem harmless, merely a verbal matter, to allow the concept of a metaphor to expand in these ways. But if metaphor is allowed to incorporate such tropes as irony, hyperbole, and meiosis on one side, and scientific and mathematical theories on the other, then the subject matter of a theory of metaphor will become so wide and disjointed that it can contain no truths that are not banalities.

THE INTERACTION OF METAPHORS

As already noted, philosophers writing on metaphors usually keep rich poetic metaphors at arm's length. 'Man is a wolf,' and 'Sally is a block of ice' are characteristic examples, with 'Juliet is the sun' about the outer limit of a daring example. One reason for this, I believe, is that attempts to analyze specific rich metaphors (for example, Browne's "light is but the shadow of God") naturally

6. This remark is restricted to the subject of this study, the figurativeness of tropes.
7. Certainly in his most recent writings.

fall into the pattern of explicating an *implicit simile*, precisely the view that most recent writers on metaphor wish to reject.

Beyond this, the expectations raised by various theories of metaphors tend not to be borne out when tested against the genuine article. This, I believe, is particularly true of the interaction or model theories of metaphor which, in various forms, dominate much recent writing on metaphors. Part of the attraction of this approach is that it seems to give metaphors a depth and significance lacking in other accounts. This depth is supposed to come from the imposition of a system of relations from one *literal* realm onto the system of relations of another *literal* realm. Calling man a wolf initiates wolf-talk about man—talk about man in wolf-words. I think that this may sometimes be right, and may account for some of the power of metaphors, but, in general, the emphasis is wrong. *The chief power of metaphor is not derived from the interaction between two distinct literal realms of discourse, but usually from the interaction of a system of metaphors themselves.* I shall try to illustrate this with a series of progressively more complex examples.

These lines come from Bessie Smith:

He was the first to boil my cabbage.
He made it real hot.
And when he put the bacon in,
It overflowed the pot.[8]

Here the subject of the sustained metaphor (what I. A. Richards called the *tenor*) is sexual intercourse, and the object of comparison (Richards's *vehicle*) is cooking, in particular, the old Southern recipe of cooking cabbage with bacon. This is certainly a remarkable achievement of transposing a set of relations from one domain to another, yet, as I read these lines, I do not find these cooking-labels illuminate the subject matter by providing a new

8. I owe this example to my colleague, W. W. Cook.

framework or *filter* for viewing it. Furthermore, the force of the *individual* metaphors fades quickly. The force of these lines lies in the match and coherent development of the metaphors themselves.

Let me try to illustrate these ideas with two, much more complex, examples. The first is Shakespeare's 73d Sonnet.

> That time of year thou mayst in me behold
> When yellow leaves, or none, or few, do hang
> Upon those boughs which shake against the cold,
> Bare ruined choirs, where late the sweet birds sang.
> In me thou see'st the twilight of such day
> As after sunset fadeth in the west;
> Which by and by black night doth take away,
> Death's second self, that seals up all in rest.
> In me thou see'st the glowing of such fire,
> That on the ashes of his youth doth lie,
> As the deathbed whereon it must expire,
> Consumed with that which it was nourished by.
> This thou perceiv'st, which makes thy love more strong,
> To love that well which thou must leave ere long.

Not trained to the task, I shall not attempt a literary analysis of this poem. I shall simply concentrate on the way its metaphors interact. Of course, a great deal will be lost by narrowing the focus in this way; for example, the match between content and rhythm in the passage "When yellow leaves, or none, or few, do hang." The metaphorical structure is not the only, perhaps not even the chief, merit of this poem, for it would be possible to take Shakespeare's system of metaphors and embed them in a perfectly awful (even if technically correct) sonnet.

In broad outline, the poet compares the poet's entering into old age, in successive quatrains, to

1. The onset of winter
2. Twilight
3. The dying of a fire.

These are all straightforward temporal comparisons, in themselves banal. The remarkable feature of the poem is that each quatrain goes on to at least double the metaphor in a complex and unexpected way. In the first quatrain, the beginning of winter is identified with trees, all (or virtually all) of whose leaves are gone, and then the *bare limbed trees* are compared with those "Bare ruined choirs, where late the sweet birds sang." The pattern is repeated in the second quatrain where twilight is picked out as that which night will take away, and then *night*, not twilight, is called "death's second self." Finally, in the most complex quatrain, the dying fire is marked by its *ashes*, and the bed of ashes is then compared with a deathbed. The quatrain then returns to the dying fire and says that it will ultimately be consumed when it has itself consumed the fuel that gives it life.

This does not exhaust the system of figurative comparisons found in this poem,[9] but it does, I think, show its general metaphorical structure. Each quatrain begins with a rather routine comparison of something with the beginning of old age. Then, within each quatrain, a second metaphor is introduced that relates the initial metaphor to death. The poem is about that time of life that will soon end with death:

> This thou perceiv'st, which makes thy love more strong,
> To love that well which thou must leave ere long.

Shakespeare's 73d Sonnet contains a number of striking metaphors and the poem gains strength from them, but, for the most part, the individual metaphors are not particularly original. The fundamental achievement of the poem is the creation and control of a metaphorical space that gives these metaphors life.

Let me illustrate this same point about metaphorical interac-

---

9. See, for example, Empson's comments on the line "Bare ruined choirs, where late the sweet birds sang," in his *Seven Types of Ambiguity*, 2–3.

---

tion by citing a more extreme example from the work of a poet now somewhat out of fashion, e. e. cummings.

> somewhere i have never travelled,gladly beyond
> any experience,your eyes have their silence:
> in your most frail gesture are things which enclose me,
> or which i cannot touch because they are too near
>
> your slightest look easily will unclose me
> though i have closed myself as fingers,
> you open always petal by petal myself as Spring opens
> (touching skilfully,mysteriously)her first rose
>
> or if your wish be to close me,i and
> my life will shut very beautifully,suddenly,
> as when the heart of this flower imagines
> the snow carefully everywhere descending;
>
> nothing which we are to perceive in this world equals
> the power of your intense fragility:whose texture
> compels me with the colour of its countries,
> rendering death and forever with each breathing
>
> (i do not know what it is about you that closes
> and opens;only something in me understands
> the voice of your eyes is deeper than all roses)
> nobody,not even the rain,has such small hands

I wish to raise only two questions about this poem: what are we to make of its last line; and what contribution does it make to the poem as whole? I think that these questions are totally unanswerable outside the metaphorical space created by the poem as a whole. Roughly, and I shall not go into this in detail, the poem is dominated by a number of interrelated leitmotivs: the oxymoron of the power that the intense fragility of his lover's eyes has to enclose him, close him, and unclose him just as spring can gently bring about these changes in a rose. This is only a first approximation to the metaphorical structure of the poem, but, even so, it excludes endlessly many readings that a mere Davidsonian nudging might produce. The small hands are not, for example, used as a symbol for stinginess, as they might be in a poem bemoaning the niggardly provisions of nature. Furthermore, from the other references to nature ("Spring . . . touching skilfully,mysteriously" and "snow carefully everywhere descending"), we know that the rain is gentle. So his lover's touch (perhaps representing the touch of her eyes) is more gentle than the touch of softly falling spring rain.

Have we then discovered what the closing line means—really means? The answer to this will depend, of course, on the plausibility of my general reading of the poem, and I realize that what I have said is both superficial and unsophisticated. But even if my general reading is plausible, or could be made plausible, I think that it would still be misleading to say that we now know what *this* line means—what *it* contributes to the poem. In isolation the line is underdetermined in content and, in some respects, unintelligible. Furthermore, this underdetermination cannot be significantly resolved by reflecting on the interaction of the system of meteorological labels (rain, snow, sleet, et cetera) and anatomical labels (eyes, hands, feet, et cetera) it contains. Of course, the literal meaning of these labels makes a difference, as does their interaction. Assigning hands to raindrops (which is simply grotesque) or treating them as hands (which is better) does produce an interaction between two systems that's of moderate interest.[10] But the significance of this line is not mainly derived from this interaction; it is fixed, instead, by the contours of the metaphorical space that encloses it. Its metaphorical meaning is determined mainly by the other metaphors in the poem, and there is no reason why *every* metaphor in the poem could not stand in this same relationship of dependence on its companion metaphors.

10. As it does in "The fog comes / on little cat feet."

To return to a point made in chapter 4, similarity claims, even the most flat-footedly literal, demand constraints on the potentially infinite range of comparisons they can invoke. Metaphors, as renegade comparisons, defy standard restraints. Yet they demand restraints from two directions. Unless the poem establishes a range of relevant comparison, metaphors will drift into the Davidsonian void, indicating nothing more than that this thing has something or other in common with that. On the other side, the poem, with its system of interacting metaphors, establishes the level of specificity at which the metaphor is to be read. In giving raindrops hands, or treating them as hands, cummings is not presenting them to us as having knuckles. There is no place in the poem for developing the metaphor in this direction.[11] This unwanted implication of the metaphor is snuffed out by its incompatibility with the dominating implications of the surrounding metaphors. The remarkable fact is that in poetry, at least in good poetry, metaphorical significance is largely achieved through mutual support and self-policing: each metaphor helps create the space in which they all have significance. A good poem justifies its metaphors.

A CONCLUDING NOTE

This work has been dominated by two themes. The first is that figurative meaning derives its force by including the respondent in a mutually recognized task of *making sense* out of what is said. With figurative predications, this involves replacing the speaker's utterance with one that squares with the context. With figurative comparisons, this involves finding ways of adjusting

---

11. The metaphorical space of a poem may support a variety of different, and sometimes incompatible, readings. This may only show a lack of control, but it can reveal a confrontation with unresolved tensions that is the mark of genius.

the context so that it squares with the speaker's utterance. This is the speech-act component of this account of figurative language, and is intended to make sense of its *rhetorical* force.

The second theme is that the underlying mechanisms of figures of speech are quite simple; they are pretty much what they seem to be at first glance. The *intellectual* and *aesthetic* force of figurative language is derived from the opportunity it provides for unlimited elaboration and sophistication. Depending upon the powers of those who use it, figurative language opens a range of possibilities from banality to genius.

Works Cited

Aristotle. *The Complete Works of Aristotle, The Revised Oxford Translation*. Ed. Jonathan Barnes. Princeton: Princeton University Press, 1984.

Austin, J. L. *How to Do Things with Words*. Cambridge: Harvard University Press, 1962.

Beardsley, Monroe. "The Metaphorical Twist." *Philosophy and Phenomenological Research* 22 (1962): 293–307.

Bergmann, Merrie. "Metaphorical Assertions." *Philosophical Review* 41 (1982): 229–45.

Binkley, Timothy. "On the Truth and Probity of Metaphor." In Johnson, *Philosophical Perspectives on Metaphor*. [*See* below]

Black, Max. "Metaphor." In his *Models and Metaphors*. Ithaca: Cornell University Press, 1962.

———. "More About Metaphor." In *Metaphor and Thought*. Ed. Andrew Ortony. Cambridge: Cambridge University Press, 1979.

Cicero. *De Oratore*. Vol. 2. Trans. H. Racham. Cambridge: Harvard University Press, 1942.

Cohen, Ted. "Figurative Speech and Figurative Acts." *The Journal of Philosophy* 71 (1975): 669–84.

Davidson, Donald. "What Metaphors Mean." *Critical Inquiry* 1 (1978): 29–46.

Empson, William. *Seven Types of Ambiguity*. New York: New Directions, 1966.

Fogelin, Robert J. "Three Platonic Analogies." *Philosophical Review* 80 (1971): 371–82.

Gombrich, E. H., Hochberg, Julian, and Black, Max. *Art, Perception, and Reality*. Baltimore: The Johns Hopkins University Press, 1972.

Goodman, Nelson. *The Languages of Art*. Indianapolis: Bobbs-Merrill, 1968.

———. "Seven Strictures on Similarity." In his *Problems and Projects*. Indianapolis: Bobbs-Merrill, 1972.

———. *Fact, Fiction, and Forecast*. 4th ed. Cambridge: Harvard University Press, 1983.

———. "Metaphors as Moonlighting." In Johnson, *Philosophical Perspectives on Metaphor*. [*See* below]

Grice, H. P. "Meaning." *Philosophical Review* 66 (1957): 377–88.

———. "Logic and Conversation." In *Syntax and Semantics*. Vol 3. *Speech Acts*. Ed. P. Cole and J. L. Morgan. New York: Academic Press, 1975.

———. "Utterer's Meaning, Sentence-Meaning and Word-Meaning." *Foundations of Language* 4 (1968): 1–18.

———. "Utterer's Meaning and Intentions." *Philosophical Review* 78 (1969): 147–77.

Hume, David. *A Treatise of Human Nature*. Analytical Index by L. A. Selby-Bigge, Second Edition, with text revised and notes by P. H. Nidditch. Oxford: Oxford University Press, 1978.

Johnson, Mark. *Philosophical Perspectives on Metaphor*. Minneapolis: University of Minnesota Press, 1981.

Lakoff, George, and Johnson, Mark. "Conceptual Metaphor in Everyday Life." *The Journal of Philosophy* 77 (1980): 453–86. Reprinted in Johnson [*see* above]. Page references are to this second source.

Lamy, Bernard. *The Rhetorics of Thomas Hobbes and Bernard Lamy*. Ed. John T. Harwood. Carbondale: Southern Illinois University Press, 1986.

Lanham, Richard A. *A Handlist of Rhetorical Terms*. Berkeley: University of California Press, 1968.

Meucke, D. C. *Irony and the Ironic*. New York and London: Methuen, 1982.

Ortony, Andrew. "Why Metaphors Are Necessary and Not Just Nice." *Educational Theory* 25 (1975): 143–57.

Prior, A. N. "The Autonomy of Ethics." *The Australasian Journal of Philosophy* 38 (1960): 199–206.

Quintilian. *Institutio Oratoria*. Vol. 3. London: William Heinemann, 1922.

Searle, J. R. *Speech Acts*. Cambridge: Cambridge University Press, 1969.

————— . "Indirect Speech Acts." In *Syntax and Semantics*. Vol. 3. *Speech Acts*. Ed. P. Cole and J. L. Morgan. New York: Academic Press, 1975.

————— . "Metaphor." In his *Expression and Meaning*. Cambridge: Cambridge University Press, 1979.

Tversky, Amos. "Features of Similarity." *Psychological Review* 84 (1977): 327–52.

Index